D0334708

La
Wet Weather Walks

Christopher Mitchell

SIGMA
Leisure

Published by Sigma Leisure – an imprint of
Sigma Press, Stobart House, Pontyclerc, Penybanc Road
Ammanford, Carmarthenshire SA18 3HP
This edition has been completely revised and updated with new maps and photographs

Originally published under the title *Rain or Shine, Walks in the Lake District Whatever the Weather* (Cicerone, 2002)

British Library Cataloguing in Publication Data

A CIP record for this book is available from the British Library

ISBN: 978-1-85058-849-8

Typesetting and Design by: Sigma Press, Ammanford, Carms

Maps: © Christopher Mitchell
Maps are based on Ordnance Survey maps: 1st edition 1:10 000 (1848-1868); 2nd edition 1:10 000 (1891-1901); 1:63 360 (1948)

Photographs: © Christopher Mitchell

Drawings: © Sarah Mitchell

Printed by: Cromwell Press Group, Trowbridge, Wiltshire

Disclaimer: The information in this book is given in good faith and is believed to be correct at the time of publication. Care should always be taken when walking in hill country. Where appropriate, attention has been drawn to matters of safety. The author and publisher cannot take responsibility for any accidents or injury incurred whilst following these walks. Only you can judge your own fitness, competence and experience. Do not rely solely on sketch maps for navigation: we strongly recommend the use of appropriate Ordnance Survey (or equivalent) maps.

To Robert and Anne

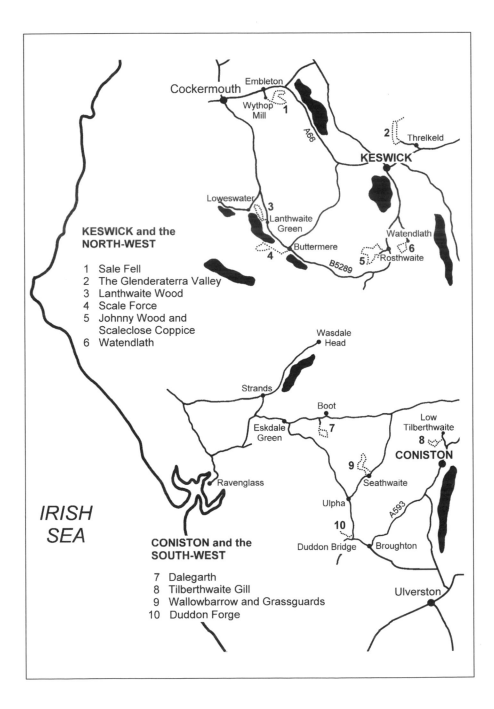

KESWICK and the NORTH-WEST

1 Sale Fell
2 The Glenderaterra Valley
3 Lanthwaite Wood
4 Scale Force
5 Johnny Wood and
   Scaleclose Coppice
6 Watendlath

CONISTON and the SOUTH-WEST

7   Dalegarth
8   Tilberthwaite Gill
9   Wallowbarrow and Grassguards
10 Duddon Forge

IRISH SEA

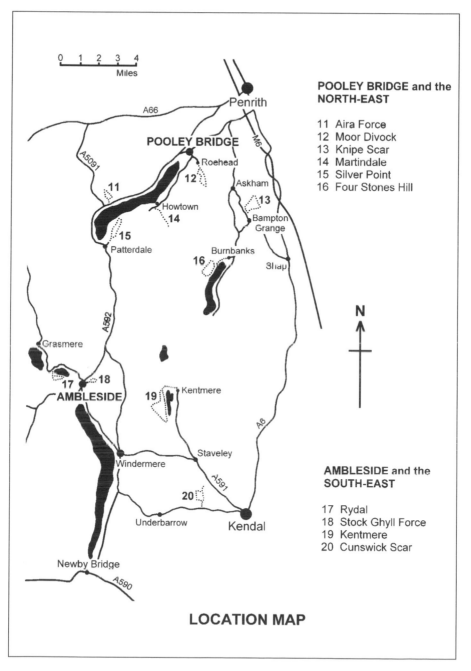

POOLEY BRIDGE and the NORTH-EAST

11 Aira Force
12 Moor Divock
13 Knipe Scar
14 Martindale
15 Silver Point
16 Four Stones Hill

AMBLESIDE and the SOUTH-EAST

17 Rydal
18 Stock Ghyll Force
19 Kentmere
20 Cunswick Scar

LOCATION MAP

Preface to Second Edition

After some of the wettest summers on record, it was fitting that I was able to complete my field notes for this Second Edition in October 2008, the wettest month of one of the wettest years in the Lake District.

It gave me the opportunity to 'test-drive' the walks in the most extreme conditions. On some days, the valleys were impassible to motor traffic. The road into Borrowdale was 3ft deep in water, yet I was still able to negotiate the narrow road up into Watendlath. I parked in the National Trust car park and then set out to check the walk – to see if the stone laid by Prince Charles was still there, to see how much of the packhorse bridge was still above water, and to re-photograph the Churn in what turned out to be a once-in-a-decade deluge.

Previous walks that same week had included Stock Ghyll Force in a rain-lashed Ambleside where even umbrellas weren't possible. It was one of those days you remember for the sheer ferocity and sound of surging water. Stock Ghyll had never looked so good!

And then there was Aira Force, where visitors were just standing, mesmerized with digital cameras, not saying a word but just staring and occasionally looking at each other in disbelief. On such a day, Patterdale was flooded and it meant re-routing the start of the walk to Silver Point, past the White Lion where a group of sheep were sheltering on the only bit of grass still above water.

What better conditions to see Scale Force, Dalegarth Force and the cascades of Measand Beck? Waterfalls were even appearing where none usually exist. I remember travelling back from Tilberthwaite into Coniston on a road that was almost a river when, across on the right, the whole fellside suddenly appeared as a white foaming torrent. A look at the map later showed it to be the aptly-named 'White Gill'.

One casualty of the First Edition was the High-Level Route on Pillar, which has been replaced with the more rain-friendly walk at Duddon Forge. All the other routes have been completely revised and updated, and the maps have been redrawn to account for any recent changes.

Chris Mitchell
October 2009

Preface to First Edition

There are hundreds of guide books on the Lake District but none of them deals specifically with the problem of where to walk and what to see in wet weather. The idea of writing such a guide suggested itself after a number of years leading field study groups on the Isle of Skye.

As in the Lake District, Skye has one of the highest annual rainfalls in the British Isles and is a magnet for hillwalkers and climbers. The problems are the same: what is there to look at when the mist comes down and you can't see further than the garden gate? How do you entertain a group of keen birdwatchers when it's been raining solidly for three days? Such problems constantly presented themselves over the years and through necessity, a strategy evolved to deal with hillwalking in wet weather.

When visibility was low and the tops were out of bounds, I found myself looking at what was close to hand. As a field biologist, that meant looking for animal tracks and signs and focusing on wild flowers and the underlying rocks. But how do you salvage something from a wet, misty day in winter when the flowers have died back and the animals are all sensibly hiding from the weather – like you feel you should be!

With so little to work on, the mind is concentrated and the eyes are focused on the smallest detail. It meant a new way of looking at a familiar landscape and extracting information that was exciting enough to make the casual visitor forget the weather.

It wasn't good enough just to identify a rock or specific plant and give it its scientific name. What made it interesting was discovering how and why things were where they were. The walks became an exercise in looking for clues and solving mysteries. The emphasis was not on covering great distances but on enjoying the journey.

It is these same techniques, gathered from over 20 years of leading wet-weather walks on Skye, that are incorporated into this Lakeland guide. Twenty walks have been chosen to cover all regions of the Lake District so that you will be able to try them out wherever you happen to be when the weather closes in.

When I first began planning this book, I was a little uncertain as to which walks would 'work'. The walks had to be fairly short, averaging between two and three miles, with little strenuous climbing. They had to be mostly low-level and preferably with sheltered sections. And most important of all, each walk had to have at least two or three novel findings that would hold people's interest – something that was unexpected and that they hadn't seen before.

The 20 walks chosen are really just a sample of what there is to see in the Lake District in wet weather. Hopefully it will encourage the reader to revisit their own favourite haunts and see them in a new light ... even in the rain!

Chris Mitchell
December 2001

Acknowledgements

This book would not have been possible without the help of many people:

I should especially like to thank my daughter Sarah for providing the pen and ink illustrations.

I am also grateful to Robert Arnold for introducing me to computer graphics which proved to be such a help in producing the detailed maps.

My special thanks go to Alan Smith (Past President and former General Secretary of the Cumberland Geological Society) for his help in identifying various geological samples and for trying to fill the many gaps in my geological knowledge. Special thanks also to the staff of the Keswick Museum and Art Gallery for their helpful advice and permission to print the photographs of the rock xylophone and fossil graptolytes. Bette Hopkins (Cumbria Sites and Monuments Record Officer) deserves a special mention for patiently sifting through her records on Bronze Age sites in response to my many telephone enquiries.

My thanks to Derrick Holdsworth (Cumbria measurer for the Tree Register of the British Isles), Edna Smith and colleagues (Natural History Museum, London), Geoff Collins (formerly Head Gardener at Inverewe), Anne Rowe and colleagues (Cumbria Record Office, Kendal), the staff at Ambleside's Armitt Museum and Library, John Hodgson (National Park Archaeologist), David Clarke and colleagues (Tullie House Museum), Geoffrey Halliday (B.S.B.I. Recorder for Westmorland and Furness, and Cumberland), Fred Slater (Cardiff University) and Tony Edwards (Macaulay Land Use Research Institute), Tony Cooper (British Geological Survey), Neil Robinson (Cumbria Naturalists Union) and Roger Putnam (formerly Warden at Eskdale OBMS); also Andrew Currie, John Roberts, Peter Holland, Mike Smith, Jed and Helen, Peter and Helen Thompson, Phil and Heather Lyon.

Thanks also to Judith and Graeme Johnston, Ralph and Jane Blain, Howard and Ruth Holden, Jean Colston, and Red and Pat Graham for all their hospitality and help with walks in their particular area; also the Warden of Longthwaite Youth Hostel for providing information on Johnny Wood and Scaleclose Coppice.

A big thank you must also go to Brad and Jean for all their recent generous help.

Above all, I thank my wife Janet for all her patience and support.

Please note
Many of the features mentioned in this book are in Sites of Special
Scientific Interest (SSSIs), Regionally Important Geological and
Geomorphological Sites (RIGS) or are Scheduled Ancient Monuments.
Please try and keep disturbance to a minimum and leave plants, rock faces
and fossil sites as you found them for others to see.

The route descriptions do not imply a right of way and, where
necessary, permission to use footpaths should be sought.

Contents

Symbol	Description	Symbol	Description
✚	Church		Lake Shore-line
◆■◆	Buildings	∼	River
Ⓡ	Refreshments	⤚	Stream (with waterfall)
Ⓣ	Telephone	⏝	Bridge
ⓦⓒ	Public Toilets	–•⌒	Wall (with gate)
Ⓟ	Public Car Park	┄┄O┄┄	Fence (with stile)
➎	Site Number	–•○⌒	Wall (with gate and stile)
⋀⋀⋀	Crags	≈	Road
Scree	Scree	- - - - -	Track
*	Archaeological Feature	⬩⬩⬩	Route
🌳	Deciduous Trees	- - - - - -	Other Paths
🌲	Coniferous Trees	[	Seat

MAP KEY

Introduction

This is not a book for the faint-hearted. I assume things are pretty bad – it's your main holiday, you've planned a week's walking in the hills and you thought you were prepared. You've packed the sun block (factor 15 at least), shorts, sun hat, designer shades – and it was great weather travelling to get here (What a sunset over Blencathra!). And now you're in Keswick and it's early morning and just look at it! Can't see the tops. Driving rain and it's blowing a gale.

Well, you've got this far and you've bought the book, so fear not – help is at hand.

First of all, it's a question of attitude. We British are pretty good at putting up with things. Bill Bryson remarked on a typically British catchphrase: 'Mustn't grumble!'

Well, of course you're going to grumble – it's been pouring down now for the past 12 hours and it's your holiday and why didn't we go to Sardinia anyway?

But relax. From now on things can only get better ...

Flooded fields at Patterdale

Equipment

What to Wear

As a hillwalker you are likely to be familiar with the latest hi-tech gear designed to protect you from the wind and rain. There is a mass of information on clothing design and fabrics and most walking magazines have test-reports on all the latest models. What I should like to mention here are some personal observations that I have found useful when facing wet weather.

Firstly, if like me you wear spectacles, you will have trouble in the rain and particularly in fine drizzle and mist. The simplest protection is to

Stock Ghyll in full flow

wear a broad-rimmed 'trilby-style' hat pulled down low under the jacket hood. A baseball hat is a reasonable alternative but will not give quite as much protection. A handful of tissues are useful to carry for wiping the lenses, but make sure they are kept dry inside a plastic bag.

In excessively wet weather, the weak spot in your clothing will be around the shoulders and neck and whatever type of jacket you wear, this is where you will feel the wet first. One way of combating this is to wear a small cotton towel like a scarf to absorb what gets through.

If it gets really windy and your hood has a loose draw-cord

adjuster, it can get annoying (and dangerous) if it starts whipping about around your face. The problem is solved by zipping the ends inside the jacket or into the breast pockets, if you have them.

If it isn't windy and you are walking low down in the valley with no fear of falling over dangerous ground and the rain is coming straight down – use an umbrella. Buy one that is a reasonable size like a golf-umbrella. It should be stronger than the town varieties, but even so, if the wind gets up, beware! *Only use it on safe, low-valley routes*, not where you could be blown off balance. When it's not in use it can be strapped to the rucksack like an ice-axe.

Footwear should suit the type of terrain. On the high fells, good quality boots are standard. Various manufacturers have now produced socks that are 100 per cent waterproof and breathable. They are expensive but they will upgrade an old pair of leaky boots. They will also transform a pair of fell-running shoes although care is needed when walking through sharp undergrowth such as gorse or brambles to avoid puncturing the built-in membrane. On low-level ground without any rock hazards, 'wellies' will guarantee you dry feet.

The Midge Problem

Midges can be a real problem from June to September when the wind drops below 5 mph and you find yourself in woodland, wet moorland or bracken. The situation is made worse when it is humid or there is fine drizzle. The most effective chemical defence is DEET (diethytoluamide) but this is a very unpleasant chemical in the concentrations that need to be used.

Once you are aware that midges are present, your nervous system will become sensitised so that anything lightly-touching the skin will be interpreted as a biting midge. A bit of self-hypnosis may help to counter this.

There are some very effective midge-hoods or, if you don't mind looking like a bank-robber, a pair of nylon tights will help, especially if pulled over a broad-rimmed hat.

Photography

Digital cameras do not enjoy getting wet. There are purpose-made waterproof covers that allow you to take photographs in the rain, although a clear plastic bag will offer some protection. A slow shutter speed used with a tripod will enable you to capture waterfalls with that soft appearance of moving water.

When photographing weather phenomena, you will need a wide-angle lens to capture a complete rainbow or halo (A word of warning: never look at the sun directly, or through a camera, as this can cause permanent damage to your eyes.). To increase the contrast of cloud formations use a polarising filter.

Weather

Cloud Types

In official MET Office language, rain comes out of low and medium-level clouds (stratus, stratocumulus or nimbostratus). Showers and thunderstorms come from low-level cloud (cumulus and cumulonimbus) whilst if you're in drizzle, you're in plain simple stratus.

The shape of the cloud will tell you what the air is doing: whether it is rising, rippling along gently, or pressing down violently. Some of the most interesting clouds are associated with cliffs, mountains and hills and are known as orographic or wave clouds. These reveal the flow of air moving over land forms. Stacks of 'dinner plates', 'flying saucers', 'almonds' and fish-shapes show that the wind has been deflected into regular waves. The cloud condenses in those sections of the wave that are rising and will appear stationary over the ground that is causing it.

Examples are seen in the north Pennines when a steady north-easterly air-flow produces the 'Helm Bar' on Crossfell. The surface waves produced by the intercepting line of hills are compressed underneath a layer of warmer air at a specific height above the ridge. The wind is called the 'Helm Wind' and its force can be felt as far west as Coniston where it funnels through the gap of Walna Sca Road.

In the Lake District itself, wave clouds are more likely to appear after a prolonged spell of cold dry easterly winds when regular stationary waves are shown by patterns in the higher clouds. But it's the wet, westerly air from across the Atlantic that concerns us here. This can produce low-level orographic clouds on those west-facing hills and cliff faces that first intercept it. Keep a look-out over Buttermere, Wastwater and Eskdale for cottonwool-like shrouds covering the peaks and ridges. This indicates very moist air and is the start of stratus cloud leading to drizzle.

Downward movement of air is seen in certain cumulonimbus clouds and indicates violent showers of rain or hail with possibly thunderstorms. The tell-tale sign is the formation of dark udder-like bulges rapidly forming and changing on the cloud's undersurface. The technical term is 'mamma' (because of their shape) – but there's nothing comforting when these appear!

'Mamma' developing under cumulonimbus cloud. Thunderstorm imminent

Lightning
Electric storms may be a dramatic sight but they can be a frightening and dangerous experience if you happen to be caught-out on a summit ridge. This happened to me on the top of Knipe Scar and my first reaction was to throw away my metal-tipped umbrella and to shelter under the limestone cliff. The modern consensus would indicate that I was right to discard the umbrella but wrong to shelter under a cliff where the currents could jump across the 'spark-gap'.

The best current advice is to get off the summit peak or ridge if possible and find an area of broken scree out in the open. Take up a crouched position sitting on top of your rucksack and keep your hands on your lap and away from the ground.

Avoid sheltering under a tree, particularly if it is tall and isolated. A cave may provide safe shelter, provided that there is a minimum 10ft/3m head room and a gap of 3ft/1m between you and the side walls.

Brocken Spectre

In certain conditions, when clouds are trapped in the valleys and the tops are in sunshine, your shadow can be cast onto the mist to form what is known as a brocken spectre (named after its frequent occurrence on the Brocken ridge in Germany). A halo or 'glory' is seen around the head formed on the same principle as a rainbow.

Rainbows

The typical rainbow is known as a 'primary bow'. If a 'secondary bow' occurs, it is wider and fainter and separated from the inner bow by a dark area of sky. There is also a rare 'reflected light rainbow', reflected more or less straight upwards from the surface of a lake where the normal rainbow meets the surface. Yet another variation can be seen when standing on a ridge or summit pinnacle, with a rain shower sweeping below into the valley, the rainbow may then approach being a complete circle.

The colours of the rainbow depend on the size of the raindrops. If the drop diameter is greater than 1mm, there will be a strong red band. If the drop size is reduced to 0.3mm, red disappears leaving orange as the first

22-degree halo around the sun predicts rain

band. When the water droplets approach 0.05mm, a white 'fogbow' appears.

Haloes
Haloes around the sun or moon are often a sign of wet weather ahead. When there are no complicating atmospheric factors, the first indication of an approaching 'low' are the ice crystals of high altitude cirrostratus forming a 22-degree halo. Depending on the conditions, various other optical effects can be seen including 'mock suns'. As the cloud-level drops, the sun appears as if through frosted glass (thin altostratus) before disappearing as the altostratus thickens, and rain is only a matter of hours away.

Public Transport
Details of bus, train and boat services operating in the Lake District National Park are available from all Tourist Information and National Park Centres or can be found on Traveline; Tel. 0870 608 2608

Using the Maps
Unlike most guide books, the routes chosen, do not lead directly to the summit ridges or cover great distances. They wander slowly from boulder to boulder, or from tree to tree. The walks may not be physically demanding but they do require concentration and careful map reading.

Each walk is described with the aid of a large-scale map and a detailed route description. It is recommended that both map and route details are studied carefully before setting out. The general Map Key is for use with all 20 route maps. Note in particular the symbols used in marking the gates and stiles.

The routes have been marked by a thick line of dashes. *This does not reflect the nature of the path. In most instances the path is wide and obvious but there are some sections where there is no clear path to follow.*

When a feature is named on the map, it is referred to in the text by using bold type (eg., **molehills**) to allow for easy cross-reference.

Site numbers represent sites of significant interest: a place to stop and examine a particular rock, plant or landscape feature... or perhaps some animal tracks and signs. The things you will encounter at each site are described fully in the route description and when this occurs you will find the site number printed in bold type: eg., **site 5**, for easy reference. A shortened description can be found alongside each map in the form of a Site Summary which can be used if necessary as a quick reminder of what you will find at each numbered site. It has been arranged so that if it is raining heavily, the book can be carried open inside a clear plastic bag or map case with the map and Site Summary side by side. This allows for quick and easy reference whilst on the move.

It is essential to familiarise yourself with the scale of each map before setting out – otherwise you may find yourself walking off the edge of the page in the first few minutes! If all 20 walks were laid out end to end, they would barely cover 60 miles. Jos Naylor, the fell-running shepherd of Wasdale, would probably complete them all in under six hours!

Most hillwalkers are used to walking at 3 miles per hour with half an hour added for every 1000ft/300m of height gained (Naismith's formula). But to see these walks at their best, it is recommended that you average 1 mile per hour which means taking at least half a day to complete the longer routes. At this speed, hillwalking changes from being a physical exercise and becomes a forensic science!

At 1 mile per hour and with frequent stops you begin to see things in a different way. That boulder you are dejectedly sheltering under has its own story to tell. Did you know, for instance, that it is used frequently by the Herdwick sheep as a rubbing post, that it fell down from the rock face behind you between 10 and 15 years ago, and is a favourite perch for wheatears, a bird that migrates here from Africa each spring? It's all in the lichen, and its secrets are just waiting to be revealed ...

Lichen Checklist

The following list provides the 'common names' (where available) and the 'scientific names' of those lichens mentioned on the walks.

Light crottle	*Parmelia saxatilis*
Dark crottle	*Parmelia omphalodes*
Cup lichens	Certain species of *Cladonia* with cup-like structures (for simplicity, I have also included those lichens that resemble matchsticks within this broad group)
Dog lichens	*Peltigera membranacea, P. polydactyla, P. horizontalis*
Map lichen	*Rhizocarpon geographicum*
Rock tripe	*Lasallia pustulata*
Mustard-colour on bird perches (acid rock)	*Candelariella vitellina*
Yellow on bird perches (limestone)	*Xanthoria parietina*
Miniature 'trees' amongst heather	*Cladonia arbuscula* and C. *impexa*
Tar-like patches on limestone	*Placynthium nigrum*

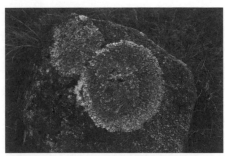

Circular colonies of crottle on High Doat

The Velcro-like barbs of dog lichen

Rock tripe on nitrogen-enriched rock

Cladonia arbuscula **(miniature trees) growing amongst heather on Moor Divock**

Walk 1. Sale Fell

For those locked in with the crowds of Keswick on a wet day waiting for Skiddaw to clear, Sale Fell offers a way out. It's not far down the road and the bus will take you to Embleton.

There is an airiness about this part of Lakeland which contrasts with the claustrophobic atmosphere of Borrowdale. Perhaps it is because you are on the edge and able to look in at all your old favourite fells from a new perspective. Perhaps it is the chance to look out across the wide expanse of coastal plain to the sea. Up here you feel the wind in your face and it is a sea breeze.

It is difficult in such bracing conditions to walk slowly. The summit has a gentle gradient covered in short springy turf. On a clear day you can see across to Scotland.

When the mist comes down, the interest is maintained by the three distinct rock formations close to the summit cairn. Wainwright mentions them as being geologically significant, but he comes away in some confusion after trying to fathom out exactly what geologists have to say (see Wainwright's comment on John Postlethwaite in The North Western Fells; Sale Fell, 11). On this walk, we shall focus on the mysterious geology of Sale Fell's summit – and hope to find the exact whereabouts of the 'beautiful rock' quoted in A.W.'s description.

Checklist

Distance	3.2miles/5.2km
Ascent	650ft/200m
Approximate time	3 hours
Maps	1:25 000 OS Outdoor Leisure 4, The English Lakes, North Western area. 1:50 000 OS Landranger 89 or 90. 1:25 000 British Geological Survey, Special Sheet NY 12, Lorton and Loweswater (S&D) 1990
Terrain	Dry underfoot for most of the way except for occasional muddy sections through Chapel Wood

Degree of shelter	Very sheltered from strong winds and rain inside Chapel Wood. Can be exposed on the remaining sections particularly if the wind is coming from the south west
Stiles	1 (optional, alongside gate)
Special considerations	Please avoid damaging the rock outcrops on the summit of Sale Fell particularly when searching for graptolytes. Fossils may be found by examining loose stones with weathered faces without having to expose fresh surfaces
Footwear	Boots
Parking	There is a small lay-by (NY185293) in front of the gate leading to the Kelswick farm road with space for three or four cars. Wythop Mill village has only limited parking space and has no refreshments or public toilets. Far better to leave the car in Keswick and catch the bus to Embleton. The Wheatsheaf Inn provides lunch-time bar meals.

The Route

From Wythop Mill the public road leads to a gate (sign: Kelswick Farm). Follow the farm road to the farm noting the white vein of quartz breaking through the shattered rock face of Dodd Crag above the bracken on your left. Below the quartz, the rock has been turned over on itself showing the extraordinary folding that led to the formation of Sale Fell (Geologists call this the 'Sale Fell – Ling Fell Anticline').

As you stand here facing north-east, looking along the spine of these hills, imagine looking along a carpet that has been pushed sideways along its left-hand edge to form a 'ruckle' down the middle. This one-sided pressure then continued to push the fold over on itself.

Just before the farm buildings, you pass a turn-off on the left with a **signpost**: 'Public Footpath Wythop Church'. Do not take this path but continue on the farm road, past the farm buildings on your left. Cross the fence at the stile (or gate) which leads onto a pleasant grassy terrace.

You are about to enter **Chapel Wood** – an ancient sessile oak woodland that takes its name from the site of the old Wythop Church **(site 1)**. Some of the church walls still remain. Here you will find a plaque and an information sheet with a photograph and a brief history of the building.

There is some uncertainty about when the church was built but there are records going back to the 16th century. It was demolished in 1865 and a lintel with the date 1673 can be seen inside the new Wythop Church of St Margaret. It is thought that the bell was hung from one of the horizontal oak branches that can be found nearby. Some of the white quartz from the vein on Dodd Crag was used in the building and several pieces can be found in the ruined walls.

A well-made track leads through a gate in a deer fence. You pass a small quarry on the left, now full of rosebay willowherb. Look for nest boxes fixed to the trees all along the right-hand side of the path. They have been put here to encourage pied-flycatchers. Around the base of the oaks, you may see tiny clusters of the white-flowering heath bedstraw.

Where the track forks, keep left. The track now climbs gently until a gate is reached that brings you out onto open fellside. If the weather is clear, there are good views to the south of Broom Fell and Lord's Seat with Skiddaw out to the east.

The path follows a wire fence which makes a dog-leg bend around groups of coppiced hazel and a hawthorn. On reaching the first hazel, notice the pale flesh-coloured fungus underneath the horizontal branches. This is **'bleeding stereum'**, a fungus that appears to weep 'blood' if you cut its surface.

After about 500ft/150m the fence makes a return dog-leg towards the path. Notice the corner-post next to the wall. It serves as a rubbing post for the local sheep and has been worn smooth on the side facing you. If you look over the fence at this point, the grass field shows signs of **'ridge**

and furrow' markings. It is difficult to give these markings a precise date. Some were made during the early mediaeval period (11th to 12th century). Others, particularly those on the higher fell sides, are thought to date from the Napoleonic Wars when marginal land was cultivated to boost the Country's food production.

After a short section of stone wall, you arrive at a gate **(site 2)**. An ancient pathway can be seen winding its way across the field. The line taken follows an old field-boundary that would once have supported a stock-proof hedge. Now that the fields have been enlarged, the only sign of the former boundary is a line of straggly hawthorns. The branches of these old trees are being pulled constantly in one direction by the prevailing south-westerly winds. When trees produce this characteristic lop-sided growth, they are often known as 'flag trees'.

Flag trees alongside ancient field boundary at site 2

The wind direction also effects the shape of the trunk. Logs cut from a tree that has grown in sheltered conditions will usually be round. But if the tree has been windblown from one direction, the logs will be oval because of the extra growth that has been added in response to the bending forces.

Wind speed increases as you travel up a mountain side and the vegetation will often show this. Notice how the lower slopes of Sale Fell are covered in bracken but as you cross the 260m contour-line this is replaced by the more wind-resistant gorse (sometimes showing signs of having been burnt to keep it under control). It is also interesting to consider why these two different plants have continued to survive in an area grazed heavily by sheep. Gorse has a physical defence of sharp spines whereas bracken uses a more subtle chemical warfare. From March until August, the bracken's green leaves produce cyanide, whilst from September onwards, the cyanide disappears to be replaced by tannic acid – and the plant is left well alone.

Approximately 230ft/70m further along from site 2, the route leaves the main path and cuts back up the slope to your left (take care at this point – the junction can be difficult to find). The narrow path climbs steadily up the side of Sale Fell between extensive patches of **gorse**. On reaching a shallow col and after passing a low **pile of stones**, the path forks. Take the right-hand path which leads you to a gap in a low broken-down wall. Once through the gap, the path crosses a series of **ridge and furrow marks** and leads to a gate in a well-kept wall before climbing gently to the summit of Sale Fell.

Immediately north of the summit the land drops into a shallow corridor running approximately east-west. This is the direction of a vein of quartz, some of which is visible 330ft/100m due north of the summit cairn. This vein of white quartz is one of many that run in a north-east to south-west direction along the anticline from Sale Fell across to Ling Fell.

From the summit of **Sale Fell** take the grassy path heading west for 330ft/100m until you reach a harbour-like wall of rock with loose, flaky slabs of stone scattered at its base **(site 3)**. This is where geologists begin to get excited. We are standing on what used to be called 'Skiddaw Slate' (now called the 'Skiddaw Group' rocks). This is sedimentary rock deposited in the sea nearly 500 million years ago making it the oldest rock in the Lake District. It was formed from various combinations of mud, silt and sand and within it are trapped very small fossils known as graptolytes.

Look on the flat surfaces of the weathered rocks for what look like delicate pencil marks about 4cm long. In fact these fossils were originally known as 'grapholites' from the Greek word graphos meaning something that has been written. The particular species found here is more easily spotted on flat weathered surfaces, where it displays a white crusty feather-like pattern. Like most delicate fossils, it is easier to see when the rock is wet.

Fossil graptolytes (courtesy of Keswick Museum and Art Gallery)

From this fossil site, head north-west for a further 65ft/20m until you reach an outcrop on the edge of the summit plateau. This is **John Postlethwaite's 'beautiful rock'** mentioned in Wainwright's description of Sale Fell's summit. This volcanic rock intruded into the Skiddaw Group at a later date (about 400 million years ago). Postlethwaite called it 'minette' but more recent geological surveys refer to it as 'kersantite'. It is coloured pink because it contains a high proportion of feldspar.

Look carefully at the large boulders. On one of the vertical flat surfaces facing north, someone has carved a name and a date. The weathering makes it difficult to see, but if the light is right it seems to read: GLEN 1941. Perhaps these unusual rocks were chosen as a final resting-place for someone's pet dog.

Before leaving the summit, walk east along the grassy corridor to examine the **quartz vein** from where a grassy path leads down in the direction of Skiddaw to reach the top wall.

Turn left at the wall until you reach a gate. Turn left again and follow the path as it keeps above the beck. Along this section, the path is a pleasant grassy terrace with good views over Bassenthwaite. Before St Margaret's Church comes into view, examine the path carefully where a bare patch of gravel breaks through the grass surface. Here, depending on the time of year, you may find what at first sight looks like bits of discarded orange peel – *Aleuria aurantia*, the rare **orange peel fungus**.

The route now contours around the north flank of Sale Fell. Where the broad path forks down to the right, take the **narrow path** that bears left without losing height. This difficult section leads across to a small **quarry** with a white cross painted on one of its rocks (Local enquiries have been unable to discover why this cross was painted here.).

The path now becomes wide and grassy once again as it crosses the north-west side of Sale Fell. At first some height is lost as you drop down to a junction **(site 4)** where a path leads down to the 'new' church. For those who do not need to return to their car at the starting point, this provides an alternative route back to Wythop Mill following the narrow road from Routenhead. If you do visit the church, look inside the porch where you will find a stone lintel from the Old Church with the date 1673 carved upon it. This was the date when the old church was rebuilt.

Stone lintel from Wythop Old Church

To return to your starting point, continue from the junction at site 4. At first, the path climbs steadily until it reaches the boundary wall that cuts across the west flank of Sale Fell. It then drops steeply down, following the wall closely to the starting point at the farm road gate.

Site Summary

1. Ruins of Wythop Old Church (NY194291)
Plaques and information sheet showing history of this demolished church. Chapel Wood contains sessile oak and pied flycatchers

2. Line of 'flag trees' (NY203294)
Old field-boundary showing effects of south-westerlies. Distinct zones of bracken and gorse caused by increasing wind exposure with altitude

3. Sale Fell summit (NY194297)
Fossil graptolytes trapped within 500 million year old mudstone. A rare intrusion of pink volcanic rock known as kersantite. An exposure of white quartz showing direction of Sale Fell-Ling Fell Anticline

4. Path junction (NY191300)
Alternative route back to Wythop Mill visiting St Margaret's Church. A stone lintel from the Old Church is on display inside

Notes
An account of graptolytes in the Lake District is given in *Lakeland Geology*, E H Shackleton (1969), Dalesman Publications.

If you wish to see specimens of local graptolytes, there is an extensive collection on display at the Keswick Museum and Art Gallery (Open Tues-Sat, 10am-4pm, Admission Free. Telephone: 017687 73263)

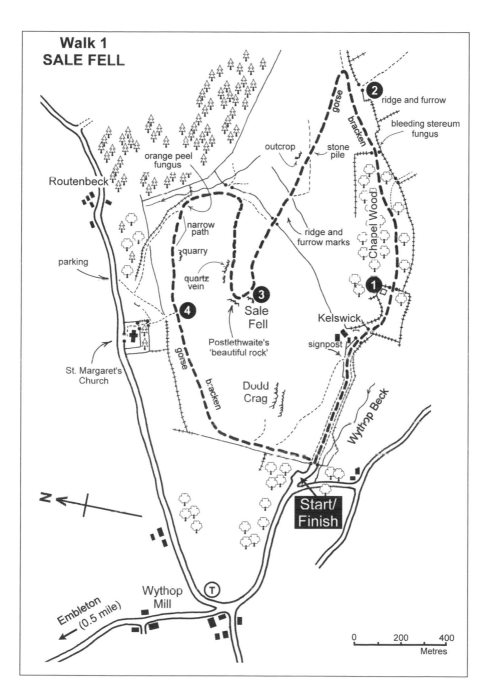

**Walk 1
SALE FELL**

Routenbeck

orange peel fungus

outcrop

stone pile

gorse

bracken

❷ ridge and furrow

bleeding stereum fungus

Chapel Wood

narrow path

parking

quarry

quartz vein

ridge and furrow marks

❶

❹

❸ Sale Fell

Kelswick

signpost

St. Margaret's Church

Postlethwaite's 'beautiful rock'

gorse

bracken

Dodd Crag

Wythop Beck

Start/ Finish

N ←

Wythop Mill

Ⓣ

Embleton (0.5 mile)

0   200   400
Metres

Walk 2. Glenderaterra Valley

Northern Lakeland is characterised by massive deposits of marine sediments known as the Skiddaw Group rocks. The smooth outline and whale-back ridges covered in purple heather reflect an underlying structure that is rather regular. Some might call it rather dull compared with the fireworks of the central volcanic landscape.

If there has been pyrotechnics here, it has all been going on quietly underground. A mass of molten rock known as the Skiddaw Granite found its way into the mudstones and changed it. As the temperature dropped, mineral deposits were formed in fractures and cavities. The centre of this activity was an area north of the Glenderaterra Valley, once well-known for its copper and lead mines.

On this walk, the granite centre is approached along the miners' track. Most of the geological events may have happened below ground but there are places where it shows itself on the surface. As you walk up the valley towards this former underground heat-source, you can see the rocks change beneath your feet. In places the dull mudstone gives way to spectacular crystal patterns. The rocks not only change colour – they even sound different!

Checklist

Distance	4.9 miles/7.8km
Ascent	900ft/270m
Approximate time	4 to 5 hours
Maps	1:25 000 OS Outdoor Leisure 4, The English Lakes, North Western area; 1:50 000 OS Landranger 89 or 90; 1:50 000 British Geological Survey, England and Wales Sheet 29, Keswick
Terrain	The miners' tracks have good surfaces with easy gradients. NB. There is no clear path leading to site 3 or between sites 4 and 7

Degree of shelter	A low-level route but with little shelter from strong winds
Stiles	2 (optional, alongside gates)
Special considerations	After a spell of prolonged rain, the stream crossings may be difficult
Footwear	Boots
Parking	Blease road end above Blencathra Centre (NY303257)

The Route

From the car park above the **Blencathra Centre**, follow the miners' track that leads north-west past a small plantation of larch. The ground is regular and the gradient gentle all the way along the west flank of Blease Fell. The colour of the path is blue-grey. You are walking on mudstones that have remained more-or-less unchanged since they were deposited in deep water about 480 million years ago.

As you continue to climb, the colour of the path changes. At the level of the disused **concrete water tanks** across to your left, flecks of white start to appear and as you approach the first gill, there are fragments that are coloured bright red and purple.

The path drops down to cross the beck and climbs up the other side, close to a bank of red scree **(site 1)**. The colours reflect the iron in the rock and the chemistry is similar to what happens when iron glazed pottery is fired in a kiln. High levels of oxygen during the firing-process produce red: low levels produce purple.

Look closely at some of the larger fragments. They are shot-through with spectacular patterns of white crystal. When viewed end-on with a microscope they are seen to contain dark cross-shaped inclusions giving them the name chiastolite (from the Greek word khiasmos, meaning cross). To the naked eye, the cross appears as a dark spot in the centre of a square cross-section of crystal.

Before leaving the gill, follow the beck upwards along its north side and then cross back over to the other bank to see the waterfall. The arrangement of crags on this right-hand side has kept a small area free of sheep. Underneath a rowan tree there is what could be regarded as a natural experiment showing what can grow in this part of Lakeland when

Chiastolite crystals from site 1

the ground cannot be reached by sheep. Notice the tall growths of heather, woodrush and hard fern. There are also bilberries, but here they are left ungrazed and have retained all their berries.

Retrace your steps back to the miners' track. In a short distance you pass an area below the path covered in **tall rushes** just before crossing a small stream. About 115ft/35m past this stream on the left is a prominent **boulder**. Whenever I see one of these isolated rocks, I feel like a detective looking for clues. Notice the mustard-coloured lichen on top (a sign of perching birds); the polished vertical edge, the grass worn away below in a muddy depression, and sometimes, the red stains – from the dye painted on the sheep that come here to rub themselves.

The path drops down to the stone-slab footbridge crossing **Roughten Gill (site 2)**. You are now much closer to the centre of the granite intrusion and the increased temperature has baked the local mudstone changing it into what geologists call 'hornfels'. The stone slabs that make up the bridge are good examples. It is hard and brittle and like metal that has been forged, it rings when tapped lightly (please avoid heavy impacts as this may cause damage). This is the same type of rock from which the famous 'rock xylophones' were made, two of which are on display in the Keswick Museum.

After crossing the bridge, turn right for about 100ft/30m along the north bank of the gill. There is evidence of a former quarry and some authorities have suggested that this may have been the site where the rock for the rock xylophones was found. The rocks show all the signs of having an interesting geology – they are covered in geologists' hammer marks! There are also freshly-broken fragments lying on the ground. The rocks are covered with black spots of a mineral known as 'cordierite' – the tell-tale sign of being heated by the underground granite.

Return to the bridge and continue following the track. You pass a stone ruin on the left before reaching another ruin further ahead on the right. Although the roof has long gone, this is a good place to shelter and have lunch if the rain is blowing across horizontally.

From this ruin, continue climbing the open fell. You cross the line of a shallow ditch – possibly a water course or **'leat'** linked with the nearby mines – and then pass two more ruined huts. Many of the large boulders scattered around this area are made of a pale crystalline rock. This is the Skiddaw Granite which produced the high temperatures and the consequent changes in the rocks we have been seeing throughout this walk.

Continue climbing steadily and aim for a solitary **rowan tree** just below the skyline **(site 3)**. Here the outcrops of hornfels appear to have a distinct grain. There are many slabs that lie scattered across the slope and new research suggests that this is the location of the musical stones.

Normally, the rocks in the Skiddaw area would split along a cleavage plane, but here above Sinen Gill, the granite has changed the rules! Here, they split along the line of the original bedding. This means that long thin slabs can be extracted. This is just what is needed if you are to construct a set of xylophone keys with a sufficient range of notes.

Cross the gill and return along its northern bank. The granite intrusion is exposed in the stream bed as a prominent rock bar which forms a waterfall. On the grass above lies a solitary boulder of hornfels. It is a classic bird perching site. Mustard yellow lichens along the top give way to leafy-grey crottle which in turn is surrounded by a luxuriant growth of **rock tripe**.

Follow the north bank of the gill and cross by the footbridge. Leave the miners' track and follow the course of Sinen Gill along its south bank to where it becomes the Glenderaterra Beck. The path along this section is indistinct and boggy. Where the beck bends to the right there is a large boulder in the middle of the stream-bed. Several metres further, the boggy path goes alongside a ridge of spoil covered in fragments of quartz. You are now at **site 4**, which is the upper adit (horizontal entrance) of the old Glenderaterra Mine, later renamed the Brundholme Mine.

Just to the left of the spoil-heap there is a collapsed tunnel entrance. One section is still intact and acts as a narrow grassy bridge across the sunken channel. The remaining masonry shows how skilfully these tunnels were made, lined with stone slabs to form an arched roof. Before leaving this ridge of spoil, see if you can spot the tiny white-flowering eyebright. The name comes from its shape which resembles an eye complete with eyelash. This plant was one of the classic herbal remedies for eye problems, an example of the 'Doctrine of Signatures': like cures like.

The path continues along the left bank of what is now Glenderaterra Beck. On your left is a mossy area with sphagnum and sundew. In front of you are two streams where Roughten Gill forms a junction with the beck **(site 5)**. Before reaching the first stream, there is another blocked adit high up on your left side. The spoil-heap is overgrown but once again there are small fragments of quartz crystals on the surface. Look carefully in front of the first stream amongst a flat area of gravel. Here you will find small fragments (less than 1cm long) of the vivid green copper ore known as 'malachite' together with brassy yellow copper pyrites: the copper equivalent of fool's gold.

Cross the two streams (the second stream is quite difficult to cross and after heavy rain you may have to accept getting wet feet at this point). Continue along the east side of Glenderaterra Beck past a ruined mine building and a third collapsed adit **(site 6)**. Once again there are remnants of a well-constructed tunnel roof. Over the top of the flooded passage is a large chunk of 'gossan', a type of iron-rich quartz that was a signal to miners that other minerals could be present and may have weathered-out nearby. On top of this you will find another traditional herb – the yellow-flowering St John's wort.

The next section is boggy but after crossing a stream, a path follows a line above the river with good views of the Glenderaterra Mine on the opposite bank **(site 7)**. This mine consists of two vertical shafts from which were driven several horizontal levels. The 'old shaft' as it was called is sited near the ruined minehead buildings and reached a depth of 30 fathoms. A second 'new shaft' was sunk a little further to the south to a depth of 39 fathoms. Both are flooded and in a very dangerous condition.

The huge mounds of spoil between the two shafts contain quartz and the heavier grey crystals of lead sulphide. Notice that there is no grass growing anywhere on this spoil even though it has been left exposed for over 100 years! The only greenery is from a sparse growth of moss that is encroaching along the sides.

The miners' track can now be joined at a bend in the river (site of **former bridge**). Look closely at the fellside opposite, to the right of a plantation of pines. This was the site of a **landslip** following heavy rainstorms on the 19th and 20th of August 2004. The debris followed the line of the stream bed and formed an extensive delta (now overgrown) below.

Continue the gentle descent passing a fenced enclosure. This is the **Blencathra Mine** which was last worked for lead in the 1870s.

On the miners' track below Blencathra Mine

The track now follows a stone wall and then crosses an open area of tall **gorse**. It eventually joins the road leading to Wesco. Almost immediately a path leads off to the left over a stile (sign: 'Footpath'). After crossing several fields, the path brings you back to the Blencathra Centre and your starting point at the car park.

Site Summary

1. Gill and waterfall (NY299270)
Red metamorphic rock containing patterns of white crystal

2. Stone-slab footbridge (NY298276)
Bridge made of hornfels (from baked mudstone). Black speckling of
rocks indicate nearby underground heat-source

3. Scattered slabs of 'musical stones' (NY304283)
Unusual rock outcrops that split along the original bedding plane

4. Collapsed adit (NY296277)
Stone-lined tunnel with quartz fragments. Eyebright growing on
spoil-heap

5. Stream junction (NY296275)
Blocked adit and spoil-heaps. Fragments of white quartz, green
malachite and yellow copper pyrite

6. Collapsed adit (NY297274)
Tunnel entrance with iron-stained quartz

7. The Glenderaterra Mine (NY297271)
Abandoned lead mine (Danger! Flooded vertical shafts). Large spoil-
heaps still bare of plantlife after 100 years of weathering

Notes
For more information on the geology of this valley see Tom Shipp (1992)
The Skiddaw Granite north of Threlkeld. In *Lakeland Rocks and
Landscape: A Field Guide*, (Mervyn Dodd, ed): pp.101-106, Ellenbank Press

Extensive details of the lead mines can be found in *Mines of the Lake
District Fells* by John Adams (1988); Dalesman Publications

For an account of the geological origins of the musical stones, focusing
on a new collecting area in Sinen Gill, see *The Origin of the Musical Stones
of Skiddaw* by Alan Smith and Bruce Yardley; Proceedings Cumberland
Geological Society, Volume 7, Part 3 (2008) pp. 263-283

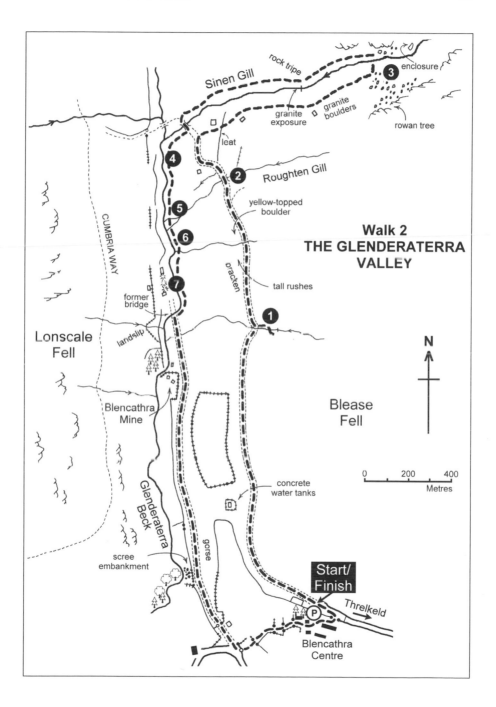

rock tripe

Sinen Gill

enclosure

3

granite exposure

granite boulders

rowan tree

leat

4

2

Roughten Gill

yellow-topped boulder

5

Walk 2
THE GLENDERATERRA
VALLEY

6

CUMBRIA WAY

bracken

tall rushes

7

former bridge

1

Lonscale Fell

landslip

N

Blease Fell

Blencathra Mine

Glenderaterra Beck

0   200   400
Metres

concrete water tanks

scree embankment

gorse

Start/
Finish

Threlkeld

P

Blencathra Centre

The Keswick Museum and Art Gallery houses an extensive collection of musical stones. The display includes a large rock xylophone built and played by the Richardson family who were thought to have gathered the stones over a period of years from Sinen Gill (For Museum opening times, see Notes: Walk 1.)

Rock xylophone built by Joseph Richardson in 1840
(Courtesy of the Keswick Museum and Art Gallery)

Walk 3. Lanthwaite Wood

Only three areas within the Lake District National Park have their own 'Special Sheet ' geology maps. They are 'Devoke Water and Ulpha', 'Black Combe' and 'Lorton and Loweswater'. It is significant that Lanthwaite Wood is included on the Lorton map. Here you will find the 'Crummock Water Aureole', with its associated veins of lead and deformed mudstones caused by a massive plug of granite that lies hidden one kilometre below the surface.

Recently, Lanthwaite Wood has drawn the attention of botanists who have just discovered a new form of green algae growing on its boundary walls. A jelly-like slime has suddenly become a major Lakeland attraction!

But you don't need to wield a geologist's hammer or a botanical hand-lens to enjoy this walk. The lakeside scenery is magnificent, to be enjoyed simply for the moment, or captured on camera. And the boat-house is the perfect place for a silhouette at sunset.

Checklist

Distance	2.3 miles/3.7km
Ascent	260ft/80m
Approximate time	2 hours
Maps	Maps: 1:25 000 OS Outdoor Leisure 4, The English Lakes, North Western area. 1:50 000 OS Landranger 89 or 90. 1:50 000 British Geological Survey, England and Wales Sheet 29, Keswick. 1:25 000 British Geological Survey, Special Sheet NY 12, Lorton and Loweswater (S&D) 1990
Terrain	The forest tracks are level and well-maintained. The rock steps between sites 5 and 6 are slippery and require care in wet weather. If you wish to avoid this difficult section, follow the forest track south to the perimeter gate where the route can be rejoined to reach site 7

Degree of shelter	Extremely sheltered inside the woodland
Stiles	4
Special considerations	Walking this route in the reverse direction is not recommended because of the difficulty in descending the rock steps at site 3
Footwear	Boots
Parking	Public Car Park at Lanthwaite Green Farm (NY159208)

The Route

From the road north of Lanthwaite Green Farm, cross the stile and follow the path that leads past the animal pens and farm buildings. Continue along the farm track, crossing a second stile and then passing through a gate into Lanthwaite Wood.

Follow the forest track for about 80ft/25m before turning off left along a narrow path that leads down to the south-east corner of the wood. A small stream runs alongside the path for a short distance before disappearing outside the wood at the end of a boundary wall (**site 1**). Drop down from the path to examine the corner of this old wall. The vertical surface facing you is covered in moss on which you will find a bright orange-coloured slime. What you see is a 'green' alga, often found in tropical rain forests. It is normally green and felt-like, not bright orange and slimy as you see here.

Green algae produce orange and red pigment in well-lit situations. These are the conditions found at this southern edge of the wood where there is less tree cover. But the 'slimy' form is completely unexpected, and so far has not been found anywhere else in Britain. Forget the ospreys on Bassenthwaite Lake – this is Lakeland's latest attraction!

The narrow path now drops steeply away from the wall towards the **boat-house** on the shore of Crummock Water. Once you have reached the shoreline forest track, turn right and continue along the lakeside track. The slope on your right was planted with European larch in the early 50s. It was felled in the mid-80s and has begun to regenerate with native oak and birch. Following this success, the National Trust is felling all the larch on the south side of Boathouse Brow. It is a fact that trees on this warmer south-facing slope grow quicker than on the opposite north-facing side of the valley. From late afternoon onwards, they also receive an extra amount of sunlight reflected off the surface of the lake.

All along this lakeside section where the ground is clear of trees, there are exposed rocks and boulders. You are walking over an area of mudstone that has been baked to a hard, glassy texture. The source of the heat was a huge intrusion of granite which geologists call the 'Crummock Water Aureole'. It lies at a depth of 0.5 mile/1km directly below where you are standing. As you walk north along the side of Crummock Water to **site 2**, you reach the edge of the area of intense heat and the surface mudstones return to their former dull state. (The

northern edge of this change-over from metamorphic to sedimentary mudstone follows a line that crosses site 4 and continues running east through Lanthwaite Gate.)

Walk along the forest track until you reach the gate at the National Trust Car Park. As you stand at the gate facing the car park, look at the ground on the right. A broad ditch leads up the slope (partly hidden in undergrowth) and ends in a basin-shaped pit. It is believed to be a **blocked tunnel**. There are a number of adits and trial tunnels in this area, all of them seeking out the vein of lead that crosses the car park and runs in a south-easterly direction across the southern flank of Brackenthwaite Hows.

The next section of the route requires careful route-finding. If you look at the map you will see a second forest track entering the wood opposite the Scale Hill Hotel. You need to cross over onto this track. The most direct way from the car park gate is to follow a narrow path that cuts through the short section of woodland just south of the blocked tunnel. The moment you reach the new track, you leave it along a narrow miners' path in a south-easterly direction. Study the map carefully here. The start of this narrow path may be difficult to find but it is marked on the 1:25 000 OS map at grid reference NY150215.

Approximately 360ft/120m along this narrow path you reach a prominent holly tree where the path turns sharp left up a series of steps cut into the rock **(site 3)**. You are now almost level with the vein of lead and you would expect the vegetation in this area to show signs of metal poisoning. The holly trees alongside the path do in fact show signs of disease and distress. Their trunks have cankerous outgrowths and their leaves are speckled brown.

The path continues to climb steeply up the rock steps alongside a wooden handrail before turning sharp right. Take great care over these old steps. They are worn smooth and are extremely slippery when wet. The path now levels off and skirts below the boundary fence and wall. There are many bilberries along this section. The trees are mostly sessile oak although there are a number of dead Scots pine below the path on the right.

Cross a stile that takes you outside the wood onto the undulating grassland below Brackenthwaite Hows. Follow the narrow, undulating path and after approximately 160ft/50m turn to the right alongside some gorse. Look carefully on the right and left of the path for dark-green

The 'pheasant' seen from site 5

mounds of grass **(site 4)**. In summer they will be speckled with the tiny white flowers of heath bedstraw. Here is one group of many ant-hills that have been built by the yellow meadow ant on this dry open grassland. The workers range in colour from yellow to golden brown. These raised mounds provide attractive perching-sites for small birds resulting in the grass on top becoming dark-green.

The path keeps to a line about 160ft/50m away from the woodland's boundary wall and passes through an extensive area of bracken. Keep a look-out for a large **isolated tree** on the left and notice how there is no bracken growing below its canopy. This tree is a favourite shelter for the local sheep and the constant trampling of the ground has kept the bracken in check.

As the path approaches the wall, you pass a decaying birch on the right and then more ant-hills covered in heath bedstraw. Look for a gap in the trees on your right **(site 5)**. This is the highest point on this section of path with fine views across the valley towards Loweswater. Look carefully at the woodland known as Holme Wood on the far hillside. It has been planted in the shape of a pheasant. The eye and neck are formed of larch. The wing coverts are mature beech. The bill, forehead and crown are Sitka spruce.

The path now loses height with bracken and bluebells on the left and fine views of Grasmoor straight ahead. Cross the wall when you reach a stile and follow a grassy path which drops steeply down to a gate that leads out of the wood. Do not go through the gate but follow the narrow path that runs inside the boundary wall.

Continue to follow the wall along to the gate where you first entered the wood and retrace your steps back to the starting point at Lanthwaite Green Farm.

Site Summary

1. **End of boundary wall (NY157206)**
   Growths of a rare orange-coloured algae

2. **Edge of the 'Crummock Water Aureole' (NY152210)**
   North of this point the metamorphic mudstone is replaced by the original sedimentary rock

3. **Rock steps (NY150214)**
   Steep steps cut into rock near lead vein

4. **Ant-hills (NY153214)**
   Dark-green grassy mound built by yellow meadow ants

5. **Surprise viewpoint (NY153212)**
   View of the 'Loweswater Pheasant'

Notes
The green algae at site 1 is *Trentepohlia aurea*, growing in a previously unknown gelatinous form. Further details regarding this specimen can be obtained from the British Museum of Natural History, London.

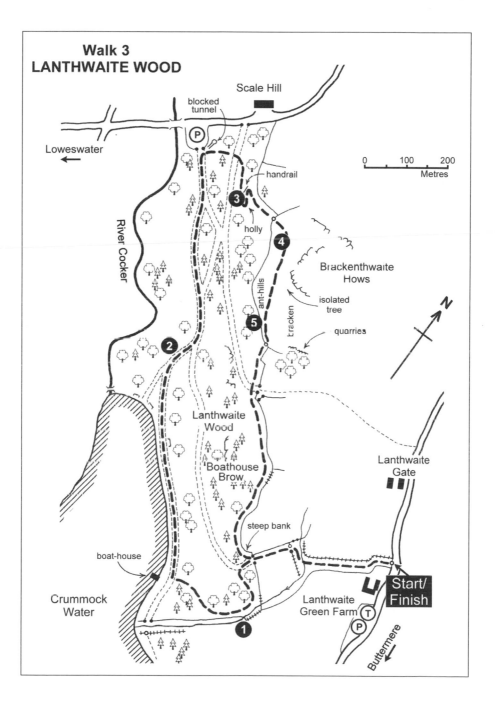

Walk 3
LANTHWAITE WOOD

Scale Hill

blocked tunnel

Loweswater

0   100   200
Metres

River Cocker

handrail

3

holly

4

Brackenthwaite Hows

isolated tree

ant-hills

5

tracken

quarries

N

2

Lanthwaite Wood

Boathouse Brow

Lanthwaite Gate

steep bank

boat-house

Crummock Water

Lanthwaite Green Farm

1

Start/ Finish

T
P

Buttermere

Walk 4. Scale Force

From Victorian times to the present, it would seem that every visitor to Buttermere makes a pilgrimage to Scale Force. The aim is to see the waterfall, and the route to it becomes just a means to that end. When guide books do mention the paths they only recall how muddy they are!

The walk described here will not escape the mud but it will show that there is more to this popular outing than just getting there and back. In fact the path takes us past two lakes and two separate waterfalls. It crosses two major areas of geology, with a detour to a hidden valley. The ground is wet but all this makes for some interesting plantlife.

At 120ft/37m, Scale Force is the longest uninterrupted plunge of water in Cumbria. The height is such that the upward currents of displaced air break up the water droplets to form a constant suspension. This results in humidity levels of 100 per cent within the narrow confines of the gorge which supports a very localised community of mosses and ferns. The 120ft drop also results in the water temperature at the base of the fall being marginally higher than at the top as the potential and kinetic energy is converted into heat.

You can of course stand below the fall without the physics and just enjoy the grandeur. After all, this is the home of the Romantics.

Checklist

Distance	4.1 miles/6.6km
Ascent	650ft/200m
Approximate time	4 hours
Maps	1: 25 000 OS Leisure 4, The English Lakes, North Western area. 1:50 000 OS Landranger 89. 1:50 000 British Geological Survey, England and Wales Sheet 29, Keswick
Terrain	The lower paths are wet and indistinct in places. The return path from Scale Force is rough and deeply eroded

Degree of shelter	The route is sheltered from strong westerly winds. The large oak trees alongside Far Ruddy Beck provides the only shelter from heavy rain
Stiles	None
Special considerations	The detour to site 8 is not recommended with young children
Footwear	Waterproof boots
Parking	Public car park next to the Fish Hotel (NY174169)

The Route

Start at the Fish Hotel and follow the famously muddy path that leads to Scale Bridge (If, after heavy rain, this path is flooded, an alternative start can be made via the bridge below **Sourmilk Gill.**).

Flooded fields by the path to Sourmilk Gill

The long straight lane with a hedge of hawthorn and willow leads you to the smooth-flowing river that connects Buttermere with Crummock Water. The path bends right towards Scale Bridge **(site 1)**. As you approach the bridge take a close look at the plants on the left of the path. As well as the familiar yellow iris growing on the water's edge, look for **apple mint** and Himalayan balsam alongside a line of large stepping stones. The bridge itself has fine growths of maidenhair spleenwort growing on the lime mortar.

After crossing the bridge, turn right. For the next few hundred metres the path becomes even wetter as it crosses three separate streams. Along this section you will find large specimens of carnivorous plants. The **sundew** grows here; its deadly leaves arranged like a rosette of red table-tennis bats. They are covered in long sticky tentacles that move very slowly to engulf any small insect that happen to land on them. You can get the same response by dropping a small piece of cheese onto one of the leaves. They are hungry for nitrogen found in the protein. The **butterwort** looks like a pale green starfish and the in-rolled leaves are

Banded Galloway cattle on the path above Crummock Water

flooded with sticky fluid that digests any unsuspecting midge in a matter of hours.

In early summer keep a look-out for the heath-spotted orchid along this left bank and as you cross the third stream look down amongst the grass for **yellow sedge**, the tops of which resemble tiny yellow pineapples.

Before reaching Far Ruddy Beck, the path forks (marked by a cairn). The original route followed the right-hand branch and crossed the beck over stepping-stones, but since the building of the wooden footbridge, this section of the 'old path' has disappeared.

Cross the footbridge and then aim off right to join the old path. Suddenly, it's as though you've gone back 100 years – when this was the main tourist route to Scale Force. If you do meet anyone, you half expect to see Norfolk jackets and long dresses! Today's visitors have been drawn by the bridge into following the higher path, leaving the lower path almost deserted.

The price for solitude is wet feet. This lower path gets even wetter and because it is out of favour, it is indistinct in places. Try keeping the same height above Crummock Water. When you are opposite **Scale Island** you may notice an indistinct fork in the path climbing gently up to the left through an area of bracken **(site 2)**. Don't take this route but keep straight on, aiming for the trees in front. Even though the path seems to disappear in the boggy ground (look out for **cranberries** in this section), keep faith and you will reach a wooden footbridge that crosses Scale Beck. Now it feels that you really have gone back in time. Half a mile away is one of the busiest paths in the Lake District and here is a route that takes you over a bridge that is almost completely forgotten.

Before crossing, it is worth making a short detour to the left following the course of the beck through the trees for a few hundred metres. The water-course divides and joins up again in a sheltered grove of dead and decaying trees **(site 3)**. This section of the beck is set down and completely hidden from above. Look closely at the birch trees. They are covered in a bracket fungus – the 'razor-strop fungus'. Its leathery surface was once used to sharpen razors. It only grows on birch and it invariably kills the tree.

Retrace your steps back to the bridge. Once over the other side you step onto drier ground onto what is in fact an island delta between the split water-course of Scale Beck. The drier ground favours colonies of the yellow meadow ant. Their characteristic nests are found in raised grassy mounds (one prominent nest is to the left of the path, just 50ft/15m from the bridge).

After crossing the next bridge, turn left until you reach and old **sheepfold**. This is a good place to practice your lichen-spotting. Most of the colonies on these rocks are perfectly circular which indicates that the granite structure has no side-to-side 'cleavage grain' for the lichen to follow. This also explains why granite walls are more difficult to construct since most of the stones are rounded and show little tendency to split into thin slabs.

Continue past the sheepfold for a further 200ft/60m. At this point, the path crosses the faint remains of an old stone wall, on top of which is an ant-hill. This slightly elevated feature has great significance for the local fox population. It is a territorial marking-post and a careful examination of the ant-hill should reveal fox-droppings.

The path now rises gently between patches of **gorse** and runs alongside a wire fence. There are some unusual contrasts in the wild flowers along this section. Look down at the rocks on the edge of the path and you will see wild thyme, whilst just to the right at the base of the fence there is sundew growing on cushions of sphagnum.

Scale Force

The path passes the junction of **Scale Beck** with its tributary, **Black Beck**, which is crossed by a footbridge. You are now on a steep tongue of marshy land between the two becks **(site 5)**. It is here that you get your first view of Scale Force pouring into its tree-lined gorge. Scale Beck on your left has had its course altered many times by the force of water. If you look down below the path you will see the course it once followed, now quite dry.

Follow the path to the footbridge and then scramble a short distance along the left side of the beck for a close-up view of Lakeland's longest waterfall **(site 6)**. At the base of the fall, there was once a trial mine – one of five exploratory levels that were dug into a band of iron deposits that runs from Floutern Tarn to Crummock Water.

Return to the footbridge to join the higher path that leads back to Buttermere. The red gravelly soil around the wall is coming from the vein of iron that runs up the left side of the gorge. The path you are about to follow is also tinged red due to the colour of the local granite. Unlike the lower path, it is deeply eroded.

As you approach Far Ruddy Beck, the colour of the path suddenly changes to a dull grey **(site 7)**. This marks the position of an isolated area of Skiddaw Slate trapped within the granite.

Unnamed waterfall in Far Ruddy Beck

Continue down to the wooden footbridge over Far Ruddy Beck. If it's raining heavily you can shelter here amongst the large oaks that grow on each side of the beck. This is the setting for another waterfall, but this one cannot be seen from the path and requires a 20 minute detour.

After crossing the bridge, walk on for about 30ft/10m and then turn off to the right, through the trees. Take care here and avoid venturing towards the edge of the ravine which is extremely steep and unstable). There is no single clear path and the climb through the trees is difficult but well worth the effort. After a steep grassy tongue covered in birch you cross an area of bracken, characterized by fallen oak and birch with their roots exposed. Approximately 100ft/30m further along from these fallen trees and across to your right, you will find the waterfall **(site 8)**. It has no name and is hardly ever visited.

Retrace your steps via site 1 back to the car park.

Site Summary

1. Scale Bridge (NY168166)
Apple mint and Himalayan balsam growing alongside large stones on approach path

2. Path junction (NY159174)
Distinct change from marshy grassland to bracken where underlying mudstone replaces granite

3. Hidden valley (NY156175)
Grove of decaying birch trees covered in razor-strop fungus

4. Stony mound on path (NY155176)
Site of ant-hill and territorial marking-area for local foxes

5. Scale Beck (NY151173)
Boulder-strewn water-course with dried-up overflow channels

6. Scale Force (NY151171)
Vein of haematite with evidence of previous mining activity

7. Change in path colour (NY162170)
Boundary of sedimentary grey mudstone trapped within the local red granite

8. Hidden waterfall (NY162168)
Spectacular falls in wooded ravine. Rarely visited

Notes
The Himalayan balsam or 'Policeman's Helmet' (*Impatiens glandulifera*) can be found in the silty deposits alongside the stepping stones before Scale Bridge. It is not a native plant of the UK. The first record of the plant in Cumbria was at Buttermere in 1921.

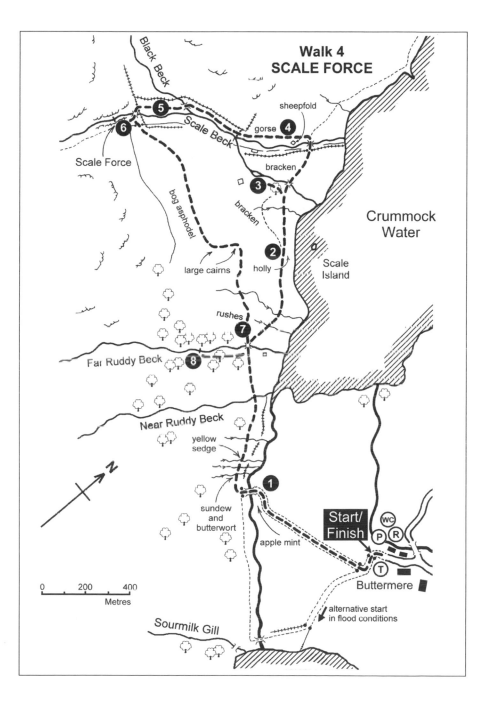

**Walk 4
SCALE FORCE**

Black Beck

Scale Beck

sheepfold

gorse **4**

Scale Force

5

6

bracken

3

bracken

bog asphodel

Crummock
Water

large cairns

holly

2

Scale
Island

rushes

7

Far Ruddy Beck **8**

Near Ruddy Beck

yellow
sedge

1

Start/
Finish

WC

P R

sundew
and
butterwort

T

Buttermere

apple mint

0   200   400
Metres

alternative start
in flood conditions

Sourmilk Gill

N

Walk 5. Johnny Wood and Scaleclose Coppice

Welcome to Borrowdale - the wettest place in England! As you travel up the valley and through its 'jaws', the annual rainfall rises dramatically from 178cm at Keswick to 318cm at Seathwaite. What are we doing here you may ask. Do we really want to walk into this? Couldn't we just sit it out in a cafe or pub or something?

Well all is not lost. This valley contains the largest area of native woodland in the Lake District and that means there is shelter beneath the trees.

Six Borrowdale woods have been identified as Sites of Special Scientific Interest (SSSIs): Castle Head Wood, The Ings, Great Wood, Lodore and Troutdale Woods, Johnny Wood and Seatoller Wood. As a group they are of international importance for their variety of ferns, mosses, liverworts and lichens for which they have been given the status of a Grade 1 site. In Seathwaite Wood alone, over 100 species of lichen have been recorded – so tread softly for you tread on a botanist's dreams!

For this walk you will be entering Johnny Wood and its outlier, Scaleclose Coppice. Both contain sessile oak that has been coppiced for making charcoal. But since this industry finished over 100 years ago, the woods have now been left to Nature.

There is an element of entering a lost world. Whilst everyone is rushing up and down the valley or clambering over the summit ridges, these woods offer a quiet refuge and shelter. The loudest noise you are likely to hear is a woodpecker looking for grubs.

Checklist

Distance	3.3 miles/5.4km
Ascent	850ft/260m
Approximate time	3 hours
Maps	1:25 000 OS Outdoor Leisure 4, The English Lakes, North Western area. 1:50 000 OS Landranger 90
Terrain	Gentle woodland paths with some short steep sections. The paths leading across High Doat are ill-defined and care is required in mist (compass recommended)
Degree of shelter	Very sheltered in the woodland sections. Exposed on the fellside below High Doat (283m)
Stiles	5 (2 optional, alongside gates)
Special considerations	The woodlands are internationally important SSSIs. Please keep to the paths. Please do not pick or disturb any of the plants. They grow here because of the especially wet conditions. A removed plant will quickly become a dead specimen. If you want a record, take a photo
Footwear	Boots
Parking	Public car park and toilets at Rosthwaite (NY257148). Parking outside the Borrowdale Institute (£2.50: honesty box). Please note that parking at Longthwaite Youth Hostel is for patrons only

The Route

The walk begins at the car park in Rosthwaite. Take the road through the village and turn left at the 'Flock In Tearoom'. Follow the road to a junction with a gate opposite (signpost: Longthwaite Youth Hostel). Follow the path across several fields to the lane and bridge which lead to the hostel grounds.

For an interesting detour to examine how glacial activity left its mark in the area, take the gravel path heading south, past the warden's house through a gate to **site 1**. On the opposite side of the river notice the high bank of loose gravelly soil with occasional large boulders. This is a glacial moraine left by the snout of a retreating glacier that once filled the Stonethwaite valley. It is the first of three terminal moraines which can be seen as three concentric mounds curving through the village of Rosthwaite. Each time the ice retreated it left a deposit of what it was carrying – similar to the lines of seaweed stranded on a beach.

The moraine that you can see on the opposite bank diverted the river coming down the Seathwaite valley and changed the course of the

Looking back over the level clearing on the ascent into Johnny Wood

Derwent at this point by squeezing it westwards. The ice and rubble held the riverbed much higher than its present level and forced the water to flow against the hard volcanic rock on the west bank. If you look at the smooth polished rock alongside the path (next to the chains that have been conveniently strung across for handholds), you will see the former riverbed. It is at least 16ft/5m higher than the present level. The constant force of water carrying small stones has left smoothed-out basins and channels in the rock.

Retrace your steps back to the hostel and take the footpath though a gate that leads along the northern boundary of Johnny Wood. After about 650ft/200m, turn left through a small gate in the fence. A narrow path leads into a **level clearing**, before climbing steeply, snaking its way through exposed tree roots and leaf-litter.

At the top of the climb you reach a gap in a wall. Notice the orange colour on the wall on both sides as you pass through the gap. This is an alga that is often seen on shaded vertical rock where people brush past. Perhaps in these situations, the moss is more easily abraded, allowing the alga to spread.

Go through the gap (marked with a yellow arrow on its south side) and follow the forest path into the heart of the wood. Look carefully for the remains of a small building on the left-side of the path **(site 2)**. The broken walls are all that is left of a charcoal burner's hut. A few metres further there is evidence of a circular clearing with a level platform of stones. This is a pitstead, where the charcoal was produced. The coppiced oak was stacked wigwam-style. A small fire was then introduced at the base and the whole structure was left to smolder slowly under a covering of turf.

The path now swings right at a second yellow waymark and follows the line of an old wall. On the south side of this wall are three rectangular areas that were **clear-felled** in the late-90s as an experiment in forest regeneration. The first site was left unfenced; the second was fenced to keep out sheep and the third was fenced against deer. At the time of writing, only the third site shows any signs of regeneration with the growth of a solitary birch.

Many of the large oaks next to these fenced enclosures have ferns growing high up on their branches. Some of the *Polypody* ferns found here are growing 33ft/10m above the ground.

The path continues through **tall bracken** until you reach the stile that takes you outside the wood. From here, turn right and then take a short detour left towards a large yew tree **(site 3)**. Yews live a long time. This one is probably over 500 years old – a young tree compared with the 2000-year-old 'Seathwaite Yew' further up the valley.

The roofless building in front is an old barn where animals were once kept. Two of the oak beams that supported the hayloft are still in their original slots set in the wall. Notice the large hazel trees nearby with fine examples of dog lichen, like white Velcro, attached to the mossy ground below.

The path leads through a gap in the wall and then climbs steadily up a bracken-clad slope. There are fine views left over to Honister Pass and behind across to Combe Gill and Grains Gill. As you follow the path, a prominent holly and an ash come into view on the skyline and the ground then dips towards a marshy pool. You pass through a gate and follow the path as it leads past a large cairn built unusually in a **sunken hollow** that frequently fills with water.

The path follows the boundary wall of the wood and then turns left climbing steeply. At first the path follows the line of the wire fence but then climbs away from the fence towards the multiple summits of High Doat (careful route-finding needed here in mist). This is the highest and most exposed part of the walk with fine views across to Castle Crag and a glimpse of Derwentwater.

The narrow path descends to a stile near a struggling hawthorn. The descent continues down a grassy slope. Look for a **large birch** growing in a wet mossy area below a wall of crags. Take a close look at its branches and examine where they join the central trunk. Here you will find a bilberry plant growing 6.5ft/2m above the ground. On the crags above are more birch, one of which looks as if it is full of crows' nests. These are called 'witches' brooms' – where a fungus has infected the buds causing the extra growth to appear like bird nests.

Take the faint grassy path north which leads down to a steep ladder-stile. Once over the stile, the path turns right down a pleasant grassy embankment with Scaleclose Gill on your left. About 160ft/50m after crossing the stile, Scaleclose Force can just be seen by carefully peering down between the birch and ash trees that line the sides of the ravine.

Continue down the grassy path for a short distance and turn left at the National Trust sign to Scaleclose Coppice. Descend the narrow gravelly path into the gill to reach the new footbridge **(site 4)**. Before crossing, notice the old pollarded ash immediately left of the bridge. It is covered in *Polypody* fern.

Continue on the path as it climbs out of the ravine until you reach the gate into Scaleclose Coppice. The narrow path climbs gently through the oak wood, keeping a few metres below the west boundary wall until reaching the top where the stream enters. You are now at **site 5**.

There is something special about this place. Here is a waterfall with no name and one that rivals any in Lakeland for atmosphere. Its wispy trail disappears into a narrow gorge filled with hart's-tongue fern, woodrush and wild garlic. This is uncharted territory in the heart of Lakeland.

Before retracing your steps, take a look at the surrounding oak trees and notice the straggly growths of moss on their bark. It is all drawn out to one side. The trailing filaments are all slanting down at an angle as if they have been pulled towards the waterfall in the ravine. This is a strange place! As you stand here, you will be sheltered from all but the westerly winds which are drawn down into the narrow ravine like a funnel. It is the only strong wind these mosses experience – a downdraft into the waterfall towards which they grow as if drawn by a magnet.

Retrace your steps back to the National Trust sign to rejoin the gently-sloping path heading back towards Longthwaite. Look for a gate and stile on the left that takes you across an area of open fields fringed with dead and decaying **ash pollards**. The path leads to the **New Bridge** across the River Derwent. Notice how the cobbles have been laid, leaving a seam down the middle.

New Bridge over the River Derwent

Continue along the riverside path and turn left at the ford to follow the lane back to your starting point.

Site Summary

1. Bend in river (NY254141)
Evidence of former riverbed diverted by glacial moraine

2. Ruins of charcoal worker's hut and 'pitstead' (NY253142)
Level circular clearing where the coppiced oak was burnt for making charcoal

3. Yew tree (NY247141)
500-year-old specimen alongside traditional Lakeland barn

4. Footbridge (NY246148)
Old ash with aerial Polypody

5. Hidden waterfall (NY247149)
Atmospheric woodland with windswept growths of moss

Notes
The glacial features of Rosthwaite are described in detail in *Glacial Features at Rosthwaite in Borrowdale* by Ken Bond, in *Lakeland Rocks and Landscape: A Field Guide* edited by Mervyn Dodd (1992); Chapter 10, Ellenbank Press.

The 'witches' brooms' growing on birch are caused by the fungus *Taphrina betulina.*

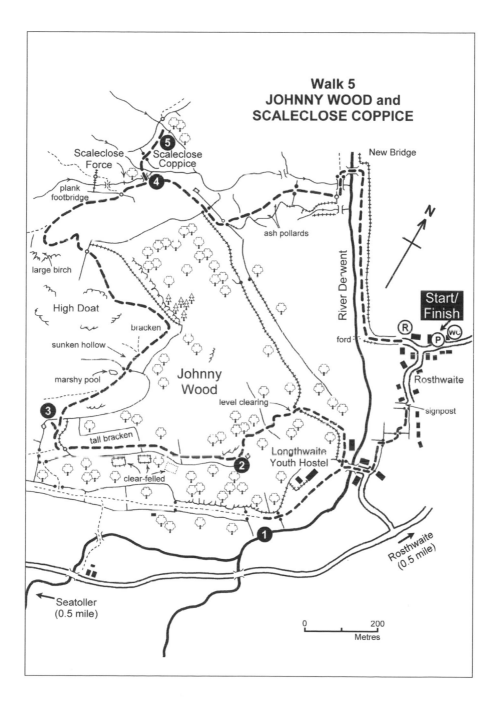

Walk 5
JOHNNY WOOD and
SCALECLOSE COPPICE

New Bridge

Scaleclose
Force

Scaleclose
Coppice

5

4

plank
footbridge

ash pollards

large birch

N

High Doat

bracken

sunken hollow

River Derwent

Start/
Finish

Ⓡ

Ⓟ

ⓌⓁ

ford

marshy pool

3

Johnny
Wood

Rosthwaite

level clearing

signpost

tall bracken

2

Longthwaite
Youth Hostel

clear-felled

1

Rosthwaite
(0.5 mile)

Seatoller
(0.5 mile)

0   200
Metres

Walk 6. Watendlath

Some parts of Lakeland are visited because of the distant views and when the mist and rain comes down there is very little to hold the eye. Watendlath is different. Even when visibility is down to 160ft/50m, there is enough here to enjoy.

The valley has been carefully managed by the National Trust who maintain those delicate countryside features that now characterise the English Lake District. Here you can expect to see stone walls, pollarded trees and a traditional working hill farm. But as this walk shows, there is much to find that is unexpected and often overlooked.

Part of Watendlath's charm depends upon the special combination of volcanic rocks, extensive peat deposits and a high rainfall. You may find equally wet ground in other parts of Lakeland but you rarely find such a variety of associated wetland plants. There may be larger waterfalls elsewhere but nothing can match the setting of 'The Devil's Punchbowl'.

This is a place that continues to attract artists and photographers

The packhorse bridge with the river in flood

seeking to find the 'traditional Lakeland view'. But there is more to Watendlath than its famous calendar image. Here is a walk especially for that rainy day when the crowds have left and the tops are out-of-bounds. Here is a chance to enjoy Watendlath at close quarters.

Checklist

Distance	2.3 miles/3.7km
Ascent	300ft/90m
Approximate time	2 hours
Maps	1:25 000 OS Outdoor Leisure 4, The English Lakes, North Western area. 1:50 000 OS Landranger 90. 1:50 000 British Geological Survey, England and Wales Sheet 29, Keswick
Terrain	Clearly-marked footpaths, mostly dry except between sites 4 and 5
Degree of shelter	A low-level walk that is well-sheltered except for the moorland crossing between sites 4 an 6
Stiles	2 (one of which is optional alongside gate)
Special considerations	The road to Watendlath from Ashness is narrow single-track with passing places and can be extremely busy mid-morning and late afternoon
Footwear	Boots
Parking	National Trust Car Park (NY276163)

The Route

Starting from the National Trust car park, make your way past Fold Head Farm to the pack-horse bridge **(site 1)**. Along with Ashness Bridge further down the valley, this is one of the most photographed sites in Lakeland. Its cobbled surface was relaid in 1995 during the National Trust's centenary year. A temporary wooden bridge was constructed alongside whilst work was underway. Look carefully on the far bank to the left of the old bridge and you will find the sawn-off foundation poles If you look carefully behind these wooden stumps on the far side, you can see two metal tubes set into the ground where the tensioning cables had been attached.

Prince Charles was invited to lay a commemorative stone in the cobble surface. It is difficult to find amongst all the other stones but look for one on the far side just before reaching a large rock breaking through the cobble surface.

Hanging from the underside of the arch is a group of ferns normally found growing on trees. This is polypody thriving in the moist sheltered conditions out of reach of the grazing sheep.

The commemorative stone

From the bridge, follow the footpath that leads left alongside Watendlath Tarn. Pass through the gate and follow the path, keeping left at the signpost to Dock Tarn. As you cross a small stream, look for spearmint at the water's edge. Another gate takes you along a path with its ancient line of pollarded ash. The fence now gives way to stone walls on which can be found specimens of cup lichen and a rather unusual moss (*Rhacomitrium lanuginosum*) normally found on high mountain tundra. The moss looks like it is covered in frizzy strands of wool which turn a characteristic greeny-grey when dry. This has given it the popular name: the 'wooly' or 'frizzy-hair moss'.

After crossing a stile, the path climbs gently along the right-hand side of a stream. Cross the stream into an open grassy area which leads across a boggy section with **sundew** on each side of the path. A little further along you cross another stream with a **hazel** growing at the bend in the wall.

The main path is indicated by an arrow-sign pointing up to the right. At this point take a short detour following the left-hand fork. You are now on a level grassy track that once led into the oak wood that covered much of the slopes on this side of the valley. The oaks were felled for timber and the soil became more acid on exposure to the high rainfall. The woodland, known as West Side Wood, regenerated itself as a birch wood.

After skirting around an open area with scattered **boulders**, the path goes between two hazels before reaching the first birch. It is part of a curious group of three trees on the left side of the path **(site 2)**. Hazel, ash and birch grow alongside each other as if out of the same base. The central ash has been pollarded. Look carefully at this ash with its fine growth of polypody. At first glance it looks as if someone has attached a hanging-basket high up in its branches. To the left of the sawn-off crown, a juniper has taken root, its seed having been deposited some years ago by a bird. Juniper trees often have different forms, sometimes growing upright and sometimes sideways. Here it is growing downwards.

Retrace your steps (about 650ft/200m) back to the path junction and follow the arrow taking you up the left side of the stream . Look for an ash next to a **rotten tree stump** on your right. The path in front of you is about to get steeper and has been carefully reconstructed with stones where it was becoming badly eroded. Look carefully to the left of the path **(site 4)**. Amongst the grass and measuring about 6.5ft/2m across is a symmetrical mosaic pattern made out of tightly-packed stones (built perhaps by one of the volunteer path workers).

The path climbs and then crosses a very boggy section before passing through a gate in a stone wall. You now meet the first of many **arrow signs** requesting walkers to avoid the former path to prevent damaging the wetland area. The path you are now following leads to a set of large stepping-stones. Do not follow the stepping-stones (they lead to Duck Tarn). Instead, take the right-hand fork at another sign **(site 4)**, following the arrow 'to Puddingstone Bank and Rosthwaite'.

This wetland area has one of the finest stands of bog myrtle in the Lake District. It is a plant that says much about the underlying geology. Its distinctive scent becomes associated with certain areas (I always remember the walk from Wasdale to Eskdale over Irton Fell where you can almost smell the change as you cross from Borrowdale Volcanic into Eskdale Granite!). Here, at Watendlath, we have crossed from fertile volcanic rock onto an area of acid gravel overlaid with peat.

The other characteristic plant of this type of wetland is bog asphodel. In late summer look for its clusters of yellow star-shaped flowers. In winter look for the dead straw-like stalks of last year's growth.

The path now follows a line of posts. After crossing a stream, keep a look-out for star sedge, so-named because of the star-shaped clusters of seeds held on the ends of its thin stems. Also along this section, you may have noticed another feature of poorly-drained peat bogs – a thin film of 'oil' covering the surface-water.

Continue over a boggy section across stepping-stones until you come alongside a steep crag on your left. To the right of the path **(site 5)** is a smooth length of rock that has been shaped and polished by ice. Because of their frequent resemblance to resting sheep, such rocks are known as roches moutonnées, only this one looks more like a stone submarine!

After crossing more stepping-stones, the path passes between two isolated hawthorns before leading through a gate. You are now at **site 6**. Notice the rushes in this poorly-drained section. In poor rural areas, the central pith of this particular plant (soft rush) was removed and dipped in animal fat to make rush lamps as an alternative to candles.

Another familiar wetland plant growing here is the lesser spearwort, which can be distinguished from the meadow buttercup by its long spear-shaped leaves. About 33ft/10m further from the gate and to the left of the path, look for a patch of bog bean, its leaves poking through the surface-water in groups of three. If you are here in May or June, you will see it in full flower – the most delicate clusters of white lace-like petals fringed with flecks of pink.

After a dry spell, this area will also show the characteristic oily film so often found on peaty ground. This coloured film is not oil but a thin layer of insoluble iron compounds. The colour patterns (Newton's rings) depend on a parallel film stretching across the surface of the water. The thinner the layer of iron, the more intense the colour that is produced.

The path now joins the main walking route from Rosthwaite to Watendlath. If the weather is clear, it is worthwhile making a short detour to climb Puddingstone Bank **(site 7)**. This provides splendid views across into upper Borrowdale with Johnny Wood and the Langstrath valley in the distance.

Rejoin the broad gravelly path leading down into Watendlath (excellent specimens of **butterwort** and sundew on the left-hand side). Notice the wire fence running parallel with and some distance below the path on the right. If it has been a wet spell, you will see the **lichens** on the tops of the posts (lichens appear more swollen and intensely coloured when wet). The bushy growths do not extend below the top line of wire. The zinc and iron from the wire kills the lichen leaving the surface below almost bare.

The resurfaced path eventually gets steeper as you pass plantations of larch on the right. The path is joined by stone walls on each side. After passing through a gap **(site 8)**, there is a view to the left of a spectacular **frost-shattered rock**, split like a cascade of falling dominoes. The rock on this side of the valley is andesite larva some of which is extremely brittle and contains small garnets.

The path leads down to the pack-horse bridge. Cross the bridge and then turn left to join the valley road. Cross the road bridge over Raise Gill and after approximately 290ft/90m look for a stile in the roadside wall on the left (the road at this point swings right).

Follow the little-used narrow path leading down from the stile to Watendlath Beck **(site 9)**. Here is a surprise feature that is often overlooked. It is a waterfall variously known as 'The Churn' or 'The Devil's Punchbowl' and in Victorian times was one of the main attractions in the area. What makes this cascade unusual are the hidden drainage channels cut into the volcanic rock. The water going into the top basin or churn doesn't all come out over the rim! Instead, it escapes through various unseen cracks to reappear under pressure in the foaming pool below.

The Churn or Devil's Punchbowl

From here, retrace your steps back to the stile, returning along the road to your starting point at the car park.

Site Summary

1. **Pack horse bridge (NY275163)**
   Commemorative stone laid by Prince Charles. Group of polypody fern growing down from underside of arch

2. **Natural birch wood (NY274155)**
   An unusual group of ash, hazel and birch with a parasitic juniper

3. **Stone mosaic (NY273156)**
   Badge-like pattern built alongside reconstructed path

4. **Path junction (NY272154)**
   Right-hand fork with sign to Puddingstone Bank. Waterlogged peat with large area of scented bog myrtle

5. **Roche moutonnée (NY269155)**
   Cylinder-shaped rock polished smooth by ice

6. **Marshy area (NY268159)**
   Rushes, lesser spearwort, sundew and bog bean in waterlogged peat

7. **Puddingstone Bank (NY267159)**
   Views of upper Borrowdale and Johnny Wood

8. **Viewpoint ((NY273162)**
   View north to frost-shattered rock face

9. **'The Churn' (NY275165)**
   Series of cascades flowing through smoothed-out rock basins

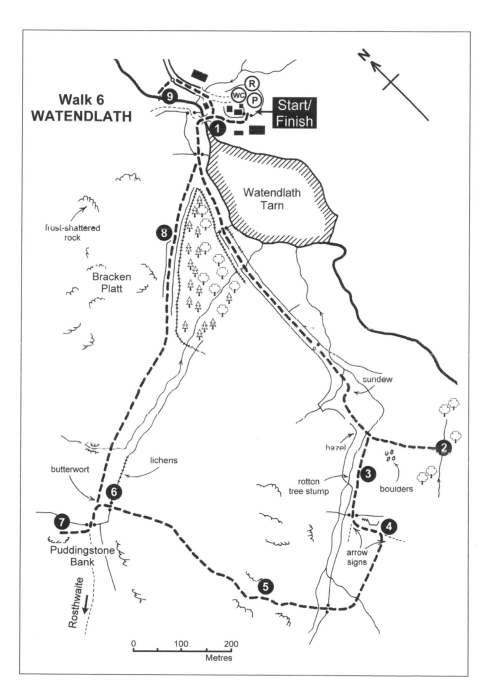

Walk 6
WATENDLATH

frost-shattered rock

Bracken Platt

Watendlath Tarn

Start/Finish

sundew

hazel

butterwort

lichens

rotten tree stump

boulders

arrow signs

Puddingstone Bank

Rosthwaite

0   100   200
Metres

Walk 7. Dalegarth

Stanley Ghyll is the perfect place for a wet day. It is sheltered and there is enough to see at close quarters to take your mind off the heaviest rainfall. Its main claim to fame is its variety of ferns, some of which grow only here and nowhere else in Cumbria.

The waterfall has a reputation as being the most beautiful in the Lake District. You could imagine entering a Himalayan jungle surrounded by exotic ferns and rhododendrons. The ravine gets narrower and more overgrown as you approach the upper falls, eventually reaching a chasm with 160ft/50m high vertical cliffs on each side.

Long after the Victorians came here to sample its 'terrors', the Outward Bound Mountain School at Eskdale used this area as a training ground. Up until the 1990s, a series of challenges were provided in and around the Ghyll to test the leadership and initiative of trainees attending the school. The area is now rarely used but the signs still exist if you know where to look.

Dalegarth Force, regarded by many as the most beautiful waterfall in the Lake District

Most of the walks featured in this book involve some element of countryside interpretation concentrating on plant and animal life. This walk is more about tracing the activity of people. At times it becomes a 'whodunit?', as the search for clues recalls the history of Outward Bound at Eskdale.

Checklist

Distance	1 mile/1.6km
Ascent	260ft/80m
Approximate time	1 hour
Maps	1:25 000 OS Outdoor Leisure 6, The English Lakes, South Western area
Terrain	Gentle woodland paths with one narrow muddy section when skirting around the top of the ghyll
Degree of shelter	Very sheltered throughout
Stiles	2 (one of which is optional alongside gate)
Special considerations	Take care with small children when approaching the platforms used for the 'Tyrolean Traverse'
Footwear	Boots are recommended (because of the section after crossing the stile above the ghyll)
Parking	Public car parks at Dalegarth railway station (NY174007) and Trough House Bridge (NY172003)

The Route

Start at the Trough House Bridge car park and follow the lane leading up towards **Dalegarth Hall**. Turn left through a gate and follow the path until you reach another gate in the wall on your left. This is **site 1**. It is just an ordinary wooden gate in a stone wall. But take a close look at the stones on each side of the opening. Look at an area about 1.5ft/0.5m up from the ground. Notice the different lichens growing here. They are bright yellow, just as you would expect on the top of a wall enriched with bird-droppings – only this is at ground level. Perhaps there is a nest in the wall just above? But this is unlikely as you are at a busy crossroads where people stop to pass through the gate. The secret lies with these yellow lichens thriving on high levels of nitrogen, from any source. To discover the source – watch your dog as you approach the wall!

Continue on past the gate following the direction of the signpost to Stanley Ghyll and Birker Fell. Go through the next gate on your left to join the network of paths leading to the waterfall. When you reach the junction in front, take the right-hand path which gently climbs alongside the west side of the beck.

Cross the first of three wooden footbridges. As the walls of the ghyll sides continue to get closer, the atmosphere gets damper. Cross the second footbridge. Everywhere you look there are ferns. Even the large oak on your left is covered in polpody, an aerial fern growing high up on its branches.

To see **Stanley Force**, you need to cross the third footbridge and climb the rock steps to a viewpoint **(site 2)**. In recent years, a landslip has made further progress difficult and there are signs warning against approaching closer to the fall. Notice the damp vertical wall of rock alongside the steps. This is also a good place to find one of the smallest of the British ferns – Wilson's filmy fern.

Retrace your steps across the third footbridge and then look for a path leading off to the left. After negotiating a **fallen tree**, the path climbs a series of rock steps. After crossing a footbridge and more steps, the path levels out and comes to a junction. Take the left fork and cross a small **slab footbridge**. After 130ft/40m, the path swings right into an area that is relatively clear of vegetation. You may find small piles of logs left in the remaining undergrowth. This is all that is left of the rhododendrons that were cleared by students of the Outward Bound School in the mid-80s. The rhododendrons are regarded as a pest species that are so vigorous, they have to be pulled out to give the native oaks a chance to regenerate.

The path now crosses some duck-boards and climbs a series of wooden sleeper-steps before reaching a gap in a line of old iron railings. Alongside the gap is a warning sign warning of the 150ft drop in front of you at the 'Rock Platform Viewpoint'. This is **site 3** – and it's here that things start to get interesting!

The first thing you notice is the magnificent Scots pine towering above the rock platform. Take care and approach the edge to look down over the narrow ravine. If you are like most visitors at this stage, you will most-likely be laid on your front with hands flat down and fingers hooked over the edge. Almost everyone who has visited this platform for the past 100 years has done just that. If you look at the edge you will see a bare strip

'In a fearful situation, a person's grip takes a very precise position' – The Rock Platform Viewpoint at site 3

of rock four inches wide (the average width of a palm) that has been rubbed clear of moss and lichen. In a fearful situation, a person's grip takes a very precise position.

There is much more to this site than at first appears, for this is where the Outward Bound School set one of its challenges known as the 'Tyrolean Traverse'. You had to get your team across the ravine using climbing rope and a length of fine string. Sometimes you had access to a few extras such as a catapult, and material for a small parachute.

How was it done? Well, the clues are still here but they need looking for. You need to look for anything unusual left behind after 50 years of attempted crossings. There must be some signs left on the rocks or on the trees or fences or somewhere. And that means looking carefully on *both* sides of the ravine.

If you look first to the right of the viewing platform you will see a birch tree growing on the edge. One of its branches juts out over the cliff below. Look at the junction of this branch with the main trunk and you will see a smoothly worn-out groove where an abseil rope has been anchored. Now look closely at the Scots pine at the back of the rock platform. At 3ft/1m and at 6.5ft/2m up from the ground there are faint traces of parallel rope burns angled downwards around the trunk.

You now need to look for evidence on the opposite side of the ravine. To get there, follow the path alongside the iron railings to a stile that takes you outside the woodland and onto the open fell. The path follows the wire fence and crosses the wooden footbridge above the falls. Once over the bridge, follow a narrow path, climbing away from the beck through dense growths of rhododendrons and birch. Take great care here, especially if the ground is wet. This section is narrow and muddy with exposed tree roots.

Suddenly you break out of the dense undergrowth and find yourself looking across to the opposite viewing platform. You are separated from the drop in front by a wooden **guard rail** and surrounded by rhododendrons **(site 4)**. Notice the area of ground you are standing on has been covered at some time with imported granite chippings to make conditions drier for the groups attempting to cross.

There is something unusual about the guard rail. If you look at the top plank you will see some strange figures carved neatly on its surface. Could this be a cryptic message that holds the key to crossing the ravine? Suddenly it feels like you've stepped into an Indiana Jones film!

Cryptic clues on the guard rail

The figures are difficult to make out but if you start from the left and work your way across you will see the four Roman numerals, 1 to 4, each one followed by an arrow pointing in a different direction. Four important steps that need to be taken in sequence to complete the task, perhaps?

So how was it done? First, the rope needs to be taken across (this is the difficult bit). It's just within throwing distance if the wind is favourable. Some groups attached the climbing rope to the fine string with a weight on the end and tried throwing it. Others used a catapult. Some have even tried to drift the thread across by parachute. Inevitably the thread became tangled in the small birch trees growing out from under the viewing platform and someone had to abseil down to retrieve it.

Once the first rope was across it had to be firmly attached. On one side, the Scots pine was used, but it was essential to attach the rope high up to allow for it stretching when loaded. On the other side, multiple attachments were used including the birch tree a few metres back from where you are now standing (look for suggestions of rope grooves at its base).

The first rope was followed by a second and a sliding transporter was then arranged so that it could be pulled back and forth along the double ropes. All that remained was to load up with each team-member in turn and pull them across. And there you have it – the Tyrolean Traverse of Stanley Ghyll.

After that, the rest of the walk seems like an anticlimax, but the Outward Bound has yet another surprise in store...

Return to the stile above site 3 and follow an indistinct path across the open fell to join the track from Low Farm back to Dalegarth Hall. Continue along the farm track (past the car park where you started) until you reach the River Esk at **Trough House Bridge (site 5)**.

After the rope-crossing of Stanley Ghyll, the cool water below Trough House Bridge looks inviting. This is where Outward Bound students took a dip in the river, jumping from the top of the bridge! You can see the exact place where they jumped (where all the lichens have been worn away). Some of their initials can be found carved on the parapet and wood fence on the same side.

The story told is that it all started in the 50s. An instructor was taking his group of students for what is known as a 'quiet walk' – a part of the course where you were taken on a gentle walk on the first day to introduce you to the surrounding countryside. As he reached the top of the bridge he said: 'follow me', and jumped over the side, fully clothed and still carrying his rucksack! The students simply followed.

Site Summary

1. **Gate in stone wall (NY172001)**
    Busy junction for walkers. Growth of lichen reflects behaviour of dogs

2. **Stanley Ghyll viewpoint (NY174996)**
    A close-up view of the waterfall. Damp rock wall with growths of Wilson's filmy fern

3. **Rock platform viewpoint (SD174995)**
    Site of the 'Tyrolean Traverse' of Stanley Ghyll. Various clues remain that show how the crossing was made

4. **East-side viewing platform (SD174995)**
    Cryptic message carved on guard rail holds the secret of the Ghyll-crossing?

5. **Trough House Bridge (NY172004)**
    Site of the Outward Bound Mountain School's legendary 'bridge-jump'

Notes
The variety of lichens found in Dalegarth Wood is unexpectedly less than is found in the Borrowdale Woods. This has been attributed to the difference in management at Dalegarth which was clear-felled in the late 1700s. See *Lichens as Pollution Monitors, The Institute of Biology's Studies in Biology no. 66*, David L Hawksworth and Francis Rose (1976); p.21. Edward Arnold.

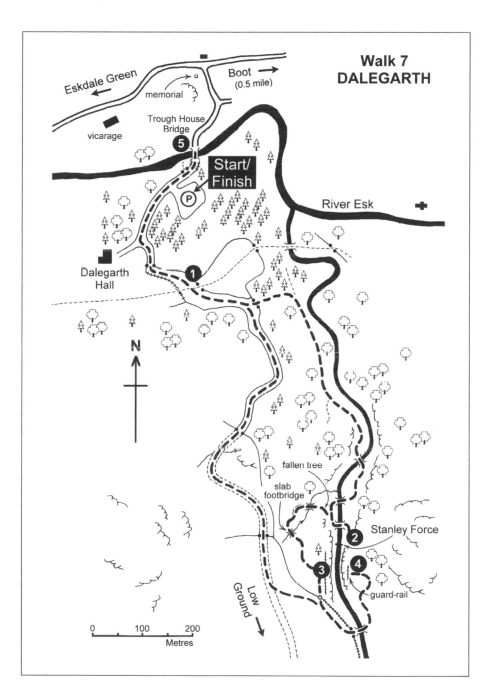

Eskdale Green

Boot → (0.5 mile)

memorial

Walk 7 DALEGARTH

vicarage

Trough House Bridge

5

Start/ Finish

P

River Esk

Dalegarth Hall

1

N

fallen tree

slab footbridge

Stanley Force

2

3

4

guard-rail

Low Ground →

0   100   200
Metres

Walk 8. Tilberthwaite Gill

This beautiful tree-lined ravine complete with its hidden waterfalls has been a favourite with tourists for many years. Former guide book writers describe magnificent gill scenery and recall how the upper ravine could be reached using a network of ladders and bridges. Although access to these upper reaches is now difficult (the ladders and bridges have long been swept away), Tilberthwaite Gill has many features that can still be explored.

At first glance it seems like a popular Sunday afternoon stroll. Then you hear the rock climbers and see the cavers with their miner's lamps and underground maps and you realise that there is more to this place than just the scenery.

This is the perfect walk for a wet day. There is enough here to concentrate your eyes downwards and to make you forget the mist-covered tops. And if the sun does happen to shine – the scenery is magnificent!

Checklist

Distance	1.5 miles/2.4km
Ascent	620ft/190m
Approximate time	1 to 1.5 hours
Maps	1:25 000 OS Outdoor Leisure 6, The English Lakes, South Western area
Terrain	Mostly well-defined paths. The approach to site 5 is narrow and ill-defined and requires care, especially in the wet
Degree of shelter	Sheltered from strong winds along lower sections. Shelter from heavy rain possible in some of the quarry caves and tunnel entrances
Stiles	None

Special considerations	The road junction to High Tilberthwaite is difficult to negotiate when approaching from Ambleside. It is far easier to head into Coniston and approach from that direction
Footwear	Boots
Parking	Low Tilberthwaite Car Park (NY306010)

The Route

From the car park at Low Tilberthwaite, cross the road and head towards the **square sheepfold** situated on flat ground above Yewdale Beck **(site 1)**. This is one of 46 folds that were designed and renewed by the internationally-renowned sculptor, Andy Goldworthy. The 'Sheepfold Project' involved the work of local authorities and groups from January 1996 until April 2003. The four walls of this particular fold contain circles of slates laid at different angles.

Return to the car park and climb the series of slate steps at the side of the spoil-heap. Notice the large number of foxgloves that have colonised

One of the slate patterns in the 'Goldsworthy Sheepfold'

these loose piles of stone. Even the sheep know that these plants are poisonous and leave them well alone. Soon the path branches off to the left into a large cave. In wet weather this is a good place to shelter.

Continue along the main path until you reach the first of four side-entrances that lead into **Penny Rigg Quarry**. The first three entrances are characterized by unusual tree formations. This first entrance has a larch that bends downwards before returning back to the vertical. Look closely along the side walls for parsley fern and wood sage.

Retrace your steps out of the entrance and continue along the main path for a short distance to the second entrance. Notice the rowan tree on the right-hand side of this rock-cutting. The roots of this tree are following the cleavage plane of the rock which is being split vertically as the roots expand. A similar event is happening at the third entrance. Here you will find a massive ash growing down the left-hand side, its main root fully exposed.

Continue on to the fourth entrance **(site 2)**. On the right-hand side of the rock passage is a white circle with a radius of 70mm. This is a colony of slow-growing lichen that adds on average just 0.5mm of fresh growth to its radius each year. Look carefully and you should see the concentric

Ash with roots exposed in the entrance to Penny Rigg Quarry

growth-rings around its outer margin. By measuring the largest colony you can work out a rough date for when this quarry entrance was cut through. A 70mm radius growing at 0.5mm a year means that it started growing on this freshly-cut rock about 140 years ago! This ties in with the date when the quarry was believed to have closed in 1875.

Continue along the main path to a junction. Take the right-hand branch that follows closely the south bank of the gill. You pass a wooden seat ('In memory of Charles Eric Samsom 1946 – 1965') from where you can see the footbridge spanning the tree-lined gorge. The path you are now following was the **line of the old water-race** that supplied power to the machinery in Penny Rigg Quarry.

Stop where the path turns right (where it leads down to a set of steep steps). At this point the water-race would have continued on in front of you in a straight line along the gill side. Strangely, it is heading higher up the gill along a course which is far too high to collect water from this section of Yewdale Beck. From where you are standing, the source of the quarry water is still a mystery.

Follow the footpath down the steps towards the wooden footbridge. There are some splendid mosses alongside these steps indicating that the air is getting progressively wetter. Most have brush-like leaves and belong to a group of mosses known as *Polytrichum* (which means 'many hairs').

Cross the footbridge. Notice the bank of vegetation immediately facing you **(site 3)** with samples of herb robert, maidenhair spleenwort and a very interesting plant with smooth, shiny leaves coloured greeny-grey with patches of pale brown. The leaf edges have projecting discs that have an uncanny resemblance to the starship 'Enterprise'! This is another form of dog lichen (*Peltigera horizontalis*) but the exciting thing about this species is that it is described by botanists as an 'old forest indicator'. It is found in ancient forests but not in newly-planted woodland. This would suggest that Tilberthwaite Gill has had a long and continuous history of tree cover.

Follow the path for a few metres and then look across to the opposite bank of the gill. Here, 33ft/10m up from the beck is the secret of the quarry's water supply. Below a rowan is the entrance to a rock tunnel **(site 4)** that extends nearly 170 ft in a straight line beneath the south bank of the gill to collect water from the upper reaches of Yewdale Beck. The line of the old water-race that once emerged from the tunnel follows the gentle gradient of the path alongside the memorial seat.

Climb the steps taking you out of the gill in a series of zigzags to a gate alongside a solitary larch. The path now makes its way up through dense **bracken** until reaching the track that climbs above the northern edge of the gill.

If the weather is poor and time is pressing, an alternative route back to the car park can be made by turning right at this junction and following the track that leads past an old **zinc adit**, joining the road at Low

The waterfall as seen from the rocky viewpoint at site 5

Tilberthwaite. If you decide to continue your ascent around the head of the gill, turn left and follow the well-engineered path along the north edge of the gill.

There are spectacular views all along this section with an almost vertical drop on your left down into the ravine below. After passing a group of juniper, birch and larch growing up from the cliff walls, you get your first view of the waterfalls. The path continues past a cairn and then a quarry path that leads off to the right. Keep straight ahead. You pass a group of windswept larches and a prominent ant-hill (yellow meadow ants) before reaching a wooden footbridge.

Cross the bridge. In front of you (west of the bridge) there is an entrance to an old copper adit with a birch growing on top. Some shelter can be found here in heavy rain. The main path climbs and then crosses a waterlogged area of peat. Do not follow this but take the narrow path above the west bank of the beck. Below you is a fault-line that contains a rich vein of copper ore. The beck has cut a deep ravine along the fault which hides a waterfall in the gorge below. To see this at its best, continue along the path, past a group of birch. Take great care along this section – the gorge drops away steeply below the path edge.

At the end of the line of birch, you reach an open boggy area with rushes. At this point, descend a short distance left to a narrow, rocky viewpoint **(site 5)**. From this airy perch, you can see the full extent of this secret waterfall, enclosed within the vertical walls of the ravine.

From this rocky knoll, climb away from the ravine along the boundary between the rushes and the bracken. Look carefully along this section for some fine growths of **fir clubmoss**, which look like miniature fir trees about two inches high. Join the main path that skirts around the top of the gill and cross the jumble of boulders over **Crook Beck**. The path now descends steadily keeping above the south side of the gill with views on the left into the tree-lined gorge below.

Look for a prominent cairn on a grassy, level area on the left side of the path. This marks the site of another adit on the right **(site 6)**. You may have noticed that most of the mine openings seen on this walk have trees growing directly on top. Perhaps after they were fenced off from livestock, young trees could become established. This particular opening supports a rowan and several juniper.

At first the path follows a fairly level section with crags on the left covered in birch, ash and juniper. It then becomes more rocky, dropping down to cross a small stream. Eventually you rejoin the quarry path that takes you back to your starting point at the car park.

Site Summary

1. **Square sheepfold (NY306010)**
   One of 46 renovated folds designed by sculptor, Andy Goldsworthy

2. **Quarry entrance (NY305008)**
   Diameter of lichen colony reveals the date when quarry was last operating

3. **Bank of vegetation (NY303007)**
   Interesting group of ferns and lichens including a 'horizontal' dog lichen

4. **Tunnel entrance (NY303006)**
   170ft/52m rock tunnel for diverting water via water-race to Penny Rigg Quarry

5. **Viewpoint (NY299008)**
   Rocky knoll with view of waterfall

6. **Copper adit (NY301006)**
   Tunnel entrance showing growth of trees on top where sheep-grazing has been restricted.

Notes

A comprehensive account of the mines in this area is given in *Coniston Copper Mines: A Field Guide to the Copper Ore Field at Coniston in the English Lake District*, Eric G Holland (1981); Cicerone Press.

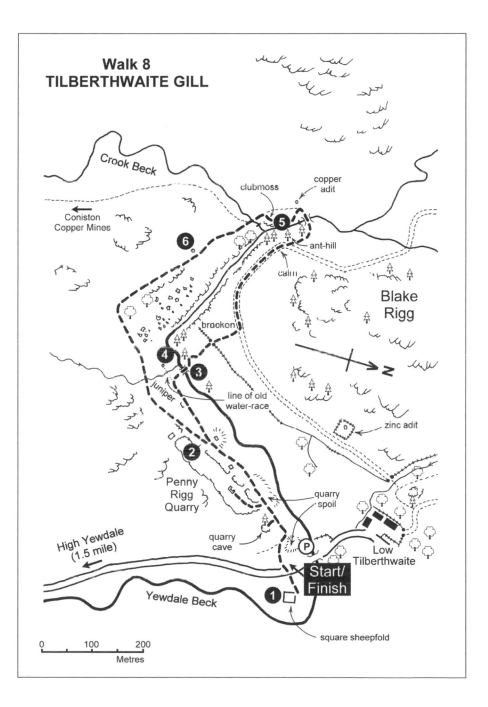

**Walk 8
TILBERTHWAITE GILL**

Crook Beck

clubmoss

copper adit

Coniston Copper Mines

5

6

ant-hill

cairn

Blake Rigg

bracken

z

4

3

juniper

line of old water-race

zinc adit

2

Penny Rigg Quarry

quarry spoil

High Yewdale (1.5 mile)

quarry cave

P

Low Tilberthwaite

Start/ Finish

1

Yewdale Beck

square sheepfold

0   100   200

Metres

Walk 9. Wallowbarrow and Grassguards

Most valley roads follow the river – but not in Dunnerdale. Motorists leaving Seathwaite may think they are following the River Duddon but the road is forced to take a detour along the tributary of Tarn Beck. The main river valley makes its way through the Wallowbarrow Gorge which can only be entered on foot. This is a special place: of quiet rock pools, ancient stepping-stones and giant wood ants.

On a raised platform on the far side of this gorge is Grassguards – once known for its wool used in the manufacture of carpets and rugs. If you look across the valley from Walna Scar Road, the area stands out as a fertile pasture. But it is not until you get up close to this ancient homestead that you see the evidence of the skill and industry of its past inhabitants. A walk through Grassguards for the first time leaves a lasting impression. There are walls here that rank with the Celtic Brochs of Glenelg and the Chambered Cairns of Orkney – only their impact is all the greater for being totally unexpected.

Checklist

Distance	3.5 miles/5.7km
Ascent	525ft/160m
Approximate time	3 to 4 hours
Maps	1: 25 000 OS Outdoor Leisure 6, The English Lakes, South Western area. 1:50 000 OS Landranger 96. 1:50 000 British Geological Survey, England and Wales Sheet 38, Ambleside
Terrain	Fairly gentle farm and forestry tracks on the approach to Grassguards. The return route involves narrow woodland paths that are steep and slippery in places

Degree of shelter	Very sheltered throughout the woodland sections. Exposed on the forestry track from Low Stonythwaite to Grassguards
Stiles	8 (for those wishing to walk with their dog, there are gates that may be used alongside most stiles)
Special considerations	The section along the side of Wallowbarrow Gorge is not recommended with young children. Any routes on the crag above or below the path along this section are dangerous and should be avoided
Footwear	Boots with good grip
Parking	There are a number of places where cars may pull off along the roadside north of Seathwaite Church (SD230963). Please note that parking outside the Newfield Inn is for patrons only

The Route

Start at the gate opposite the 'School House'. After crossing the concrete footbridge over Tarn Beck, follow the path straight ahead through an oak and birch woodland until you drop down to join the River Duddon. If the river level is low you will pass a flood channel along this section resembling a dried-up riverbed. When the river level is high, many of the trees along here are left stranded on their own narrow island.

Continue alongside the river until you reach the **stepping-stones** made famous by one of Wordsworth's sonnets. There are many stepping-stones across the Duddon but these are some of the oldest and probably date back to the 13th Century.

About 33ft/10m further, between the path and the river edge, you pass a mound of chewed-up leaves. If you look carefully, especially when the weather is warm, the leaves will appear to be moving. This is a nest made by the wood ant, *Formica lugubris*. These giant ants are thought to have invaded the Wallowbarrow woods after being introduced at Duddon Hall to feed pheasants. You don't want to be standing here too long.

The path leads on through a gate in a wall to **site 1**. This is the

AB's commemorative plaque

Memorial Bridge, mistakenly believed to be a memorial to the Royal Air Force. As you walk between its carefully constructed parapets, notice that the north-facing side supports a healthy growth of wall rue thriving on the lime-mortar. This shade-loving fern avoids the direct sunlight and struggles to grow on the drier south-facing side.

When you reach the middle of the span, look over the left side to see the initials A.B. carved on a stone plaque. Over on the opposite side, there is a mysterious rune-like carving that could almost have stepped out from a Tolkien novel. On careful inspection and allowing for the fact that you are looking at it upside down, you can see the Greek letters *alpha* and *omega* enclosing a star-shaped symbol.

Just before leaving the bridge, on the inside of the right-hand wall, there is another carved plaque:

'BUILT BY W. GRISENTHWAITE FOR A.F. AND R.A.F. 1934'

'A.F.' was Aida Foster and 'R.A.F.' was a Greek scholar, Robert Allason Furness. They were respectively the daughter and friend of 'A.B.', Aida Borchgrevink (born Starr). Aida Starr had married a Norwegian and after the 1914-18 war lived in Duddon where she died in 1931. It sounds very complicated but look again at the carvings on the outside of the bridge. The Greek letters intertwined with a symbol of her maiden name was specifically chosen to commemorate A.B.'s life: beginning and ending as a 'star' in the eyes of her friends.

If the river is not in flood, turn right on crossing the bridge, and carefully make your way down to the water's edge to examine the underside of the arch. It has been constructed of cast concrete and the lime is slowly leaching out as the rainwater drips through. Notice the stalactites that are forming under the arch.

Stalactites growing in sheltered conditions under the bridge

From the bridge take the woodland path leading west away from the river. After approximately 650ft/200m you reach a gate into open parkland where the path contours around a pleasant grassy terrace. Follow the waymarked path through several farm gates taking you past the gardens and exotic wildfowl of **High Wallowbarrow (site 2)**. The red stones in some of the farm buildings come from an intrusion of red microgranite that extends north-east from here in a straight line parallel with the gorge. Keep to the farm track as it climbs steadily along the west bank of **Rake Beck** below the rock-climbing pitches of Wallowbarrow Crag. Once above the tree-line there are extensive views behind of the lower Duddon Valley with Caw and Stickle Pike on the skyline.

Follow the track over the exposed fell passing **Low Stonythwaite** on your left. Notice the thick bank of *Polytrichum* **moss** on the right of the path. Try spotting the two vertical bands of quartz on **Hollin How**. The holly trees that gave it its name are not so obvious, but a little further along, the rowans of **Rowantree How** can still be found.

The track takes you on down into **Grassguards (site 3)**. The first thing you notice are the walls. These are no ordinary walls. Some sections are 13ft/4m high and in places are 13ft/4m thick! They are beautifully constructed tapering towards the perfectly-levelled coping-stones. Some appear to serve little function other than to act as a tidy store for stones cleared from the fields.

As you cross the ladder-stile, you are able to look down on the tops of these walls. The coping-stones are covered in a type of moss that is normally found on exposed mountain tops. This plant is a good indicator of humidity and can predict a forthcoming change in weather conditions. The side facing a drying wind turns from green to grey as the leaf tips are transformed into hoary-white wisps. This distinctive appearance gives it the name 'frizzy-hair moss'.

After turning right through a gate, you enter a more open area with a wire fence on one side **(site 4)**. Lichens are extremely sensitive to pollution, particularly from metals like zinc and iron. Look at the fenceposts where the galvanised wire has been stapled to the wood. Lichen thrives on the top but immediately below the first line of wire, where the zinc and iron have drained down, the wood is clear of all growth – as if it has been scraped clean. One of the best examples can be seen in front of you – on the seventh post back from the stone ruin.

Continue on past the farm houses (A sign indicates an alternative route for those wishing to avoid the farmyard.). Cross the footbridge over **Grassguards Gill**. Once over the bridge, the path leads to a gate. Don't go through the gate but turn right and take the path following the line of the gill. After a gate, the narrow path becomes steeper involving a tricky descent over wet and slippery rock.

The atmosphere gets progressively darker as you enter a mature beech wood and eventually reach the gorge in what seems like perpetual twilight. In front of you are the notoriously **Fickle Steps** complete with wire hand-rail. If you are planning to cross the river at this point after a period of heavy rain, these stepping-stones can be impassable. The water level can rise very quickly, particularly if held back by a high tide in the Duddon Estuary coupled with a westerly gale.

The route continues along the west bank of the **River Duddon**. Cross the fence at the stile and notice the bracken and grass trapped in the wire on your left showing the level of the river when it's in flood. Continue over the footbridge and then over a boggy section with **duckboards**. You are surrounded by bog myrtle and enclosed by trees. Eventually the path climbs as it follows the line of the fence. Take **care** along this section. The

The extraordinary walls of Grassguards

path is narrow in places and the gorge drops away steeply below.

There are more boggy sections before descending a narrow path with exposed tree roots. The yellow flower along the side of the path is cowwheat.

After crossing a stile and then a gap in a broken wall, the path crosses a line of block-scree along the foot of **Wallowbarrow Crag**. The views up towards the towering cliffs and pinnacles are dramatic and in summer you will hear the alarm calls of peregrines and ravens as they compete for space in the air above.

As you progress across the scree, the boulders get larger, some providing a welcome shelter under their leaning faces **(site 5)**. What has caused this jumble of fallen rock and why has it developed on this side of the gorge and not on the other? Both sides of the gorge are made of andesite lava but here on the west bank there is a weaker layer of sandstone sandwiched between the denser volcanics. The combination of heavy rock resting on a weak foundation causes an unstable cliff face. Andesite splits along three planes, each at right angles to the other, and so it breaks into the rectangular-shaped boulders that you see in front of you.

After crossing a stile in an old wall, the path becomes much easier and leads back through the woods to the memorial bridge. Cross the bridge and follow the path straight ahead, keeping the wall on your right. The path leads across several boggy sections before bringing you back to Tarn

Site Summary

1. Memorial footbridge (SD224964)
Greek and Norwegian connections with carved signs and inscriptions

2. High Wallowbarrow Farm (SD221963)
Band of red microgranite seen in path and farm buildings

3. Grassguards' walls (SD224976)
Some of Lakeland's finest stone walls: 13ft/4m thick!

4. A fencepost puzzle (SD224978)
Why does no lichen grow below the top line of wire?

5. Boulder field (SD225967)
Heavy volcanic rocks resting on weak foundations. Aerial displays of ravens and peregrines

6. Weir and sluice-gate (SD229962)
Nearby water-wheel generated electricity for Seathwaite before valley was connected to the National Grid

Notes
More information on the area can be found in *Walks around Furness and the Duddon* by Ian Brodie (1985), Dalesman Publications.

The northern or hairy wood ant (*F. lugubris*) is also found in Borrowdale around Lodore and Ashness Bridge. In Victorian times, colonies of these ants were often introduced into pheasantries to provide food for young birds.

The moss on the right of the path after passing Low Stonythwaite is *Polytrichum commune*. The moss found on the top of the walls at Grassguards is *Rhacomitrium lanuginosum*.

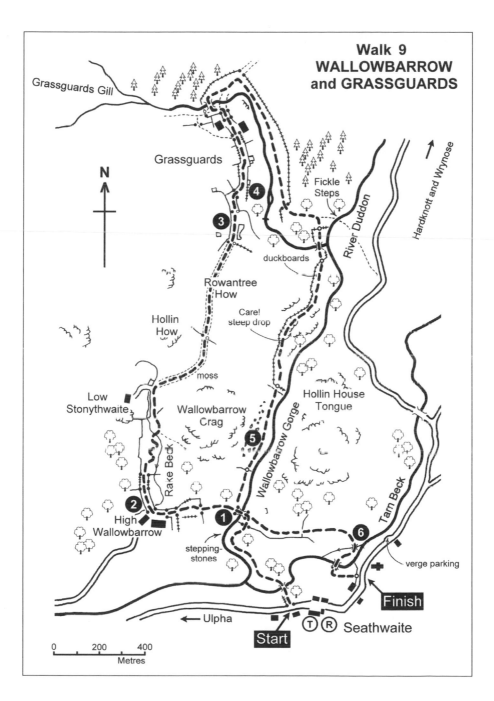

Walk 9
WALLOWBARROW
and GRASSGUARDS

Grassguards Gill

Grassguards

N

Fickle
Steps

River Duddon

Hardknott and Wrynose

duckboards

Rowantree
How

Care!
steep drop

Hollin
How

moss

Low
Stonythwaite

Wallowbarrow
Crag

Hollin House
Tongue

Wallowbarrow Gorge

Rake Beck

Tarn Beck

High
Wallowbarrow

stepping-
stones

verge parking

Finish

← Ulpha

Start

Ⓣ Ⓡ Seathwaite

0   200   400
Metres

Nearly there! The final section crossing the field opposite Seathwaithe Church

Beck **(site 6)**. The small weir across the beck was built along with the sluice-gate and water channel to redirect the flow to a horizontal water wheel. The electricity generated supplied the nearby inn and farm buildings before the valley was connected to the 'mains' in 1951.

Follow the beck and cross over the wooden footbridge into a grassy field. On the right-hand side of the path is a low outcrop of volcanic rock that has been smoothed and polished by glacial action. Bear left and follow the sign to Seathwaite Church, finally making your way through an extremely-narrow stone gap-stile to join the valley road.

Ravens above Wallowbarow Gorge

If you have time, visit the Newfield Inn to see a fine example of flow-banded slate that came from the Walna Scar Quarries. It was used in the flag-stone floors of the public bar and in many of the nearby houses. The pattern of complex parallel banding is unique to the Duddon Valley.

Walk 10. Duddon Forge

Take the road from Broughton and head towards the traffic lights at Duddon Bridge. Cross the bridge, and turn right. The first time you come this way you will almost certainly miss it. Here, hidden amongst the woodland, is the most complete example of a charcoal-fired blast furnace in England.

Vast amounts coppice were cut to supply the charcoal and once the forge was at full heat, it would remain running for up to nine months at a time. This was just one of many forges that operated in the area. The iron ore and limestone were dug locally but the demand on the woodland was such that charcoal was brought in from the west coast of Scotland. Eventually it became more profitable to move the whole production process to the woods of Argyllshire.

This walk is the perfect antidote to a wet day. As well as the extensive archaeological interest, the sheltered oak, hazel and birch coppice is the ideal place for a fungus foray. On a clear day, the track beyond the wood

Duddon Iron Works. The thick walls of the furnace dominate the site; the iron store and charcoal sheds extend up the slope to the left

has extensive uninterrupted views across the Duddon Estuary, with Blackpool Tower ever-prominent on the skyline.

Checklist

Distance	2.5 miles/4km
Ascent	850ft/260m
Approximate time	3 to 4 hours
Maps	1: 25 000 OS Outdoor Leisure 6, The English Lakes, South Western area. 1:50 000 OS Landranger 96
Terrain	Dry woodland paths with some steep sections. The path to the quarry is well-defined, mostly on grass, with a gentle gradient. There are no clear paths on the fellside on Barrow
Degree of shelter	The route is well-sheltered throughout the woodland section
Stiles	None
Special considerations	The detour onto Barrow is not recommended in mist
Footwear	Boots
Parking	Car park (SD197883). Not obvious as it requires opening a gate by the roadside

The Route

Start from the car park and make your way to the restored site of the Duddon Furnace **(site 1)**. An information board describes the layout and gives historical details. The water driving the waterwheel was taken from the River Duddon via a **'head race'**. The renovated houses opposite the furnace were once workers' cottages and stables.

Follow the path that takes you around the end of the **charcoal stores** until you come to some piles of cut logs stacked along the right-hand side **(site 2)**. Here, growing on the rotting wood, you will find magnificent specimens of candlesnuff fungus (*Xylaria hypoxylon*). They look like burnt candle wicks complete with grey ash at their tips. The logs also support large specimens of honey fungus – leathery-brown toadstools with thin, curving stems.

After crossing a driveway, the narrowing path crosses a stream and then leads past two water tanks. There are rhododendrons on each side. The path now forks just before a tributary. Follow the white waymark pointing right which takes you across the remains of an old stone bridge.

The path now climbs along a stony section, into the oak woodland with exposed tree roots. A **rock buttress** separates the cascading stream from the path, which now climbs steadily alongside a dried-up stream bed dotted with patches of the 'scaly male fern' (looking like giant green shuttlecocks). This is a delightful section following an old wall covered in

Candlesnuff fungus growing at site 2

moss. You pass a large beech and an oak where the path and the wall swing to the right. If you look over the wall at this point, you will see an old trackway which leads up to a charcoal burner's hut **(site 3)**.

The path now becomes narrower and swings left and then right, passing a plantation of larch and young Norway spruce, before leading to a gate in a well-constructed wall. The narrow path now climbs through an area of bracken and brings you into an open grassy space with a group of stones in the middle. One of them is split, leaving the smaller piece alongside like the end sliced off a loaf of bread. To the left is a **rocky knoll** – an oasis of bell heather amongst the encroaching bracken. If the weather is clear, it is worth scrambling to the top for the first views of the Duddon Estuary.

**A view of the Duddon Estuary from site 4
with the town of Barrow-in-Furness on the skyline**

From the **split stones**, head north west and follow the wall to a gate with a blue waymark. Follow the boggy path, keeping the wall on your left. The views looking back now open out over to Barrow in Furness. You pass a **sheepfold** and then a gate.

The main path turns left to follow the **'head dyke'** – the wall separating the lower fertile land from the open fell – but if the weather is good, take a detour at this point to climb the little-known fell named **Barrow**. The first rocky outcrop is a favourite lookout perch for the local crows **(site 4)**. It is covered in rock tripe, mustard-yellow *Candelariella* and bird pellets. The remaining rock surface is colonised by green-yellow map lichen, indicating this is volcanic rock with a high silica content.

Now make your way upward between boulders and outcrops. There are no walkers' paths here, only sheep tracks to follow. You reach a false summit before descending to a shallow depression with a small **tarn**. From here, climb up and choose your own summit outcrop **(site 5)**. For the effort involved this is one of the best viewpoints in south Lakeland with extensive views of the Duddon and Coniston fells to the north-east, and the ever-changing tidal flats of the Duddon Estuary glinting to the south.

The descent is best made by retracing your steps to the pool and then following the shallow (mostly grassy) depression cutting down through the tall bracken towards the head dyke. At the wall, turn right and follow the path past a **sheep pen**. You are now approaching the area marked 'cave' on the OS Outdoor Leisure Map. The large spoil heap indicates that this was once an important slate quarry (site 6) supplying the nearby farms.

Amongst the loose piles of spoil, look for foxgloves, herb robert and English stonecrop. The quarry entrance has an overhanging ash tree. At the end of the quarry is a deep cavern filled with water. About 13ft/4m back from the rim of this hollow, on the west side-wall, just above ground-level, there is an unusual moss with crinkly leaves (*Mnium undulatum*). It is a species that is particularly shade-tolerant and can grow in almost complete darkness.

The path that you followed to reach the quarry was once used to transport the slate. On your return journey, look carefully at the sides of the path for evidence of wear from a sled or cart. Approximately 33ft/10m past the sheep pen you will find the first of several **rock grooves** that have been worn into the rock by a pair of wheels or sled runners.

Continue following the wall until you reach the gate below site 4 and then retrace your steps back to the starting point.

Site Summary

1. **Duddon Ironworks (SD197883)**
   Recently restored charcoal-fed blast furnace

2. **Log piles (SD196882)**
   Fine examples of candlesnuff fungus and honey fungus on decaying wood

3. **Charcoal burners' hut (SD193880)**
   Ruined hut and ancient trackway associated with charcoal production

4. **Rock outcrop (SD187884)**
   Look-out perch for crows with rock tripe, bird pellets and map lichen

5. **Viewpoint (SD185887)**
   Summit outcrop on Barrow with extensive views of the Duddon Estuary

6. **Cave (SD184886)**
   Narrow quarry entrance and water-filled cavern. Unusual moss growing on shaded rock wall

**Walk 10
DUDDON FORGE**

Thwaite Yeat

sheep pen

rock grooves

spoil

cave

gorse

Barrow

tall bracken

Wrayslack

tarn

0   100   200
Metres

sheepfold

→ Z

rocky knoll

split rock

bracken

Furnace Wood

Thwaites Fell

rock buttress

'head race' (former route)

weir

charcoal stores

A595(T)

Whicham

furnace

River Duddon

Duddon Bridge

Start/
Finish

Ulpha →

Broughton

Walk 11. Aira Force

Seasoned walkers of the Lakeland fells may dismiss Aira Force as an artificial pleasure garden that is best left to families with prams or car-bound tourists wishing to stretch their legs. Think again – especially on a wet day.

Even if there was nothing else to see but the waterfall, this walk would leave a lasting impression. It is busy and there are families (but not with prams) and the paths and steps are artificial; but the first time you see Aira Force, the cynicism disappears. Even the purist must admire the bridges.

Stand behind the iron rails looking up to where the main fall shoots under the top bridge and the clichés are forgiven. The view is literally breath-taking! The sheer volume of water pouring 70ft/21m into a confined space causes air to be displaced sideways and upwards. The spray is forced out to meet you and the noise is deafening. If there are rainbows, the first colour will be orange, reflecting the small size of the water droplets found in the swirling mist.

Coming face to face with such elemental forces is all the more shocking following an approach that has been so contrived. You are led to expect a Victorian water-garden where nature has been tamed and put on display. But in effect, the ordered paths and exotic trees serve merely to highlight the savagery that awaits you!

Checklist

Distance	1.4miles/2.3km
Ascent	260ft/80m
Approximate time	1 hour
Maps	1:25 000 OS Outdoor Leisure 5, The English Lakes, North Western area
Terrain	Well-maintained footpaths and steps throughout the entire walk
Degree of shelter	Excellent shelter from wind, rain and sun
Stiles	None

Aira Force

Special considerations	The ideal walk for a wet day
Footwear	Ordinary shoes or trainers
Parking	National Trust Car Park (NY401201)

The Route

This walk begins at one of the busiest car parks in the district. Choose a wet day and if you are arriving by car in the height of the season, arrive early morning or evening to guarantee a place.

Make your way through the gap alongside the **National Trust Information** building. Follow the iron railings and pass through the gate with the National Trust's acorn emblem on each side. The broad path has a wire fence on the right behind which is a fine specimen of one of Lakeland's native hardwoods – the durmast or sessile oak.

Continue on the broad path and pass through the gate in a stone wall. Suddenly it becomes darker as you enter a Victorian arboretum. There are two yew trees, one on each side of the path and then the first exotic tree is seen on the left **(site 1)**. To the left of a wooden balcony and a fallen hollow trunk is a tall evergreen named grand fir (*Abies grandis*). Everything about this tree is big. The leaves are like those of a Christmas tree only four times larger. When bruised they smell of oranges.

Cross the bridge and follow the path to the right around the edge of an open **grassy space** and stand at the gap in the low iron railings **(site 2)**. In front of you across the grass about 330ft/100m away is a line of some of Lakeland's tallest trees. Starting on the left, there is a monkey-puzzle tree or Chile pine (*Araucaria araucana*); to its right and behind is the much rarer Himalayan fir (*Abies spectabilis*); then the tallest in the group, a Douglas fir (*Pseudotsuga menziesii*). The next tall tree on the right is the European silver fir (*Abies alba*) and the group finally ends with another monkey-puzzle tree. [Incidentally if you really want to impress (or lose!) your friends, the scientific name of the Douglas fir is taken from the surname of the Scot who discovered it and is pronounced 'mingiz-i-eye'].

After some steps and crossing a bridge over the river you will find a young pine to the right of the path **(site 3)**. This is a Monterey pine (*Pinus radiata*). Although it is very sensitive to frosts, it is one of the most wind-resistant pines, helped by the extremely wide-spacing of its needles.

Now the path begins to climb up a series of steps and bears left. Just before the path forks to the right, you pass an old ash with woodpecker holes. Keep left and you will come face-to-face with a real giant and one of the most remarkable-shaped trees in the Lake District **(site 4)**. Here is a Sitka spruce (*Picea sitchensis*) with a circumference of over 20ft/6m, making it one of the largest specimens in the British Isles. (The largest is in Devon with a circumference of 27ft/8m). At some stage, a side branch grew out horizontally and then decided to grow vertically like the spout of an up-turned coffee pot. On a smaller side-branch directly above the path, there is a bird's nest.

The giant Sitka spruce at site 4

A few metres further down from the path is another giant, this time a particularly fine specimen of silver fir, so-named because in sunshine the foliage has a silvery gleam due to white patches on the back of the needles. At this point you can almost be forgiven for forgetting the main reason for coming here – to see the waterfalls!

Continue along the path as it makes its way down past some large oaks, with their roots exposed. Look for wood sage and cow-wheat along the path side. A series of steps takes you down to a stone bridge **(site 5)**. You know something is different here from the noise and the fine mist in the air. Look over the right-hand parapet to see hart's-tongue fern and *Polypody* growing on the bridge stonework, thriving in the perpetually damp air. As you leave the bridge, notice the patch of wild garlic just to the left of the path.

A few steps further and you arrive at the muddy viewing platform.

Site Summary

1. **Grand fir (NY400203)**
   Unusual fir with large leaves that smell of oranges

2. **Tall tree viewpoint (NY401203)**
   Chile pine, Himalayan fir, Douglas fir and silver fir can be seen
   looking north across grassy clearing

3. **Monterey pine (NY401203)**
   Unusual pine with needles in groups of three

4. **Sitka spruce (NY401204)**
   One of the largest specimens in Britain with a circumference of over
   20ft/6m

5. **Lower stone bridge (NY399205)**
   View of Aira Force. Hart's-tongue fern growing on bridge masonry

6. **Upper stone bridge (NY399206)**
   View looking down onto Aira Force

7. **High Force (NY401208)**
   Narrow rock channel spanned by wooden footbridge. Double
   cascades within narrow ravine

8. **Silver fir (NY400204)**
   The tallest tree in Cumbria at a height of 160ft/50m

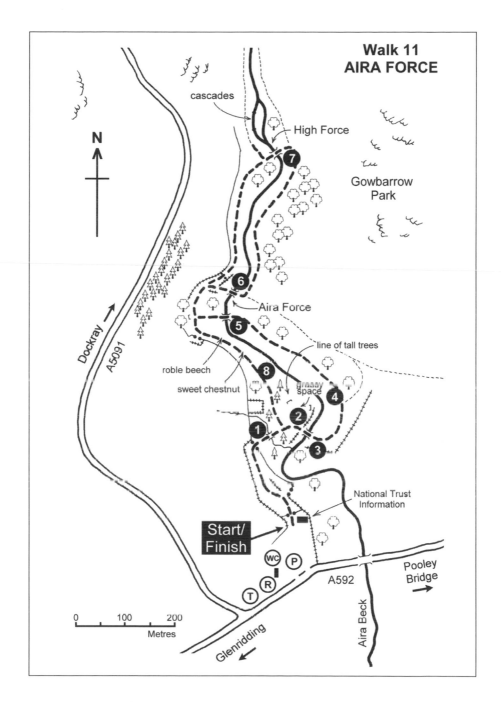

Walk 11
AIRA FORCE

cascades

High Force

N

Gowbarrow
Park

7

6

Aira Force

5

line of tall trees

roble beech

sweet chestnut

8

grassy
space

4

2

Dockray

A5091

1

3

National Trust
Information

Start/
Finish

WC P

R

T

A592

Pooley
Bridge

Glenridding

Aira Beck

0   100   200
Metres

Aira Force can now be seen pouring through the stone arch of a distant bridge spanning the narrow gorge.

Climb the steps and then bear round to the right to join the path that leads to the top bridge **(site 6)**. As you look down directly over the fall, try spotting the honeysuckle growing amongst the rocks on the left.

After crossing the bridge, follow the path left along the east side of the river. After approximately 990ft/300m, at a bend in the river, the flowing water can be seen to have undercut the rock walls that enclose it. Continue along the path a further 330ft/100m until you reach a wooden footbridge spanning a narrow rock channel. This is High Force **(site 7)**. After crossing the bridge, follow the path along the west side of the river to see the double **cascades** set within a narrow ravine.

Retrace your steps back to the bridge. Your route now takes you on (past the path that leads down to the stone bridge above Aira Force), now following the wire boundary fence. Continue on (past the junction down to the lower stone bridge) keeping straight ahead past the seat with a view of the Force. The view is getting progressively less each year due to the increasing foliage. Further along the path you have an unexpected view over a sheep-pen out over the boundary fence across to Place Fell. After descending more steps, the path levels out. At this point, to the left of the path, you will find an unusual southern-hemisphere tree – a **roble beech** (*Northofagus obliqua*) – introduced into Britain from Chile in 1902.

The growing conditions here are perfect and the huge trees along this section reflect this. First we pass a **sweet chestnut** (*Castanea sativa*). The top has been sawn off and the base shows signs of fungal attack. Alongside are two towering Christmas trees or Norway spruce (*Picea abies*). Two fallen tree trunks spanning the river will help locate the site. A little lower down towards the river edge is a silver fir **(site 8)**. This tree is 160ft/50m high and is the tallest tree in Cumbria.

The path now drops gently and becomes very dark, passing by a group of yews on the left. All that remains now is to join the path that leads around the edge of the grassy space and retrace your steps back to the car park.

Walk 12. Moor Divock

On a hot sunny day, I wasn't prepared for this. At times, I felt like an archaeologist exploring the tombs of Egypt complete with wide-brimmed sun hat and parasol. And then I was strolling down the wide fairway of what could have been a golf course complete with hidden bunkers. We are of course, in the Lake District just a few miles out from Pooley Bridge, but this is totally unexpected.

Moor Divock is a Bronze Age site and most of what is here has been well-documented. There are robbed burial cairns, stone circles, cairn circles, and standing stones. Archaeologists have also identified two parallel lines of stones – the Askham Fell Stone Alignment – used possibly for ceremonial purposes associated with the many funeral sites.

And then there are the shake holes – following definite lines like wartime bomb craters. At first you don't see them, and then you find one and you are drawn further on to the next, wondering how deep and if it will be full of water.

What makes this place different is that all this interest is hidden. When you set off walking from Roehead you wonder what all the fuss is about. There is nothing but flat open moorland. Even when you have reached the first cross-road after half a mile, there is nothing. Another half mile and still nothing. And then it begins...

Checklist

Distance	4miles/6.4 km
Ascent	360ft/110m
Approximate time	2 to 3 hours
Maps	1:25 000 OS Outdoor Leisure 5, The English Lakes, North Eastern area. 1:50 000 OS Landranger 90. 1:250 000 British Geological Survey 54N 04W, Lake District
Terrain	WARNING – The lack of reference points on this flat open moorland can make route-finding difficult and this walk is not recommended in misty conditions.

Terrain (cont'd)	The moorland track from Roehead is wide and easy to follow but once you leave the track, there are no clear paths leading to the archaeological sites or shake holes. Even when conditions are clear, great care is needed when searching for the described sites. Most of them cannot be seen until you are 'on top of them' It may help to count the number of paces that you take when venturing away from the main track (one large stride equals approximately 3ft/1m) and relate this carefully to the positions of the sites on the map It is also recommended that the appropriate OS map (and a compass) is used in conjunction with the route details described here and that both are studied carefully before setting out
Degree of shelter	A low-level walk but with no natural shelter
Stiles	None
Special considerations	The main path across Moor Divock is a popular Sunday outing and parking may be difficult at Roehead. All the Bronze Age sites visited are Scheduled Ancient Monuments. It is an offence to disturb or deface them or to use a metal detector within 6.5ft/2m of their boundary
Footwear	On a dry day, trainers or walking shoes are adequate
Parking	There is room for up to 10 cars along the roadside at Roehead (NY479236). At peak periods an alternative would be to approach from Helton, parking on the roadside verge at NY497214

The Route

From Pooley Bridge take the road heading south-east past the church to the roundabout. Follow the sign to Hill Croft and continue on to Roehead where the road ends. Pass through the gate (sign: Barton Fell Common, No Cars or Motorcycles beyond this point) and follow the wide moorland track up a gentle gradient. At first there are few visible features except for a number of small grassy paths leading off through the bracken.

Continue straight ahead and notice how the track begins to divide the vegetation: bracken on the left, grass and heather on the right (bracken prefers to grow on dry ground and this is the key to understanding this area). After reaching some **gorse**, look closely to the right of the path for an isolated boulder. This is a volcanic **erratic** left here during the last Ice Age. This is the first feature you meet in this flat landscape. The local bird population is aware of this and makes full use of it for perching and territorial display. Almost every stone you encounter from now on has a yellow top caused by lichen growing on the bird-droppings.

The start of the moorland track across Moor Divock

The gently-rising track leads to a crossroads and a large **cairn**. After approximately 1300ft/400m you reach the next junction marked by a block of stone less than 3ft/1m high. This is an old **boundary stone** made of soft Penrith sandstone.

About 500ft/150m past the boundary stone look for a group of stones above the bracken about 260ft/80m from the track on your left. This is **White Raise Cairn (site 1)**: a Bronze Age burial chamber that has been robbed. The central stone compartment or cist has had the lid removed and discarded alongside. The rock is white limestone. Notice the familiar yellow lichen where birds have perched and notice also the less-familiar patches of black as though the rocks have been splashed with tar. This is yet another lichen but this one grows specifically on limestone.

Rejoin the track. After 800ft/250m you pass a junction where a path to Askham leads off to the left. More stone monuments are hidden along this left side. In fact, as you walk in this southerly direction, most of the Bronze Age sites are just to the left of the track and most of the shake holes are on your right. You may also have noticed that most of the bracken is on your left with grass and heather to the right.

The key to these divisions lies with the geology and one explanation may involve the boundary lines of the underlying rock. From the moment you reached the first shake hole, the road follows the edge of the carboniferous limestone that forms the north-east boundary of the Lake District. The bracken tells you what is underneath for it grows only on well-drained soil. As you move to the broken edge of the limestone, the underlying volcanic rocks begin to restrict the surface drainage. It is in this intermediate area where you find the shake holes. Beyond this there are the usual volcanic rocks overlaid with peat.

After passing the Askham turn-off, and if the weather is clear, it is worth while exploring more carefully this left-hand side of the moor **(site 2)**. The stones in this area are known as the **Askham Fell Stone Alignment**, (National Monument Number 22526). This is how they are described in the National Records:

'[The monument] is divided into two separate areas by a natural sink hole. The easterly part includes two virtually parallel alignments of irregularly spaced stones 6m-9m apart, oriented approximately north west - south east, and running for a length of 70m. There are 15 stones in the northern line and seven stones in the southern line. Some of the stones remain upright while others appear to have fallen. The maximum height of the stones is 0.3m. At the south east end there is a slight bank up to 0.1m high and 1m wide that continues the southern-most alignment of the stones for a further 8 m. The western part of the monument continues approximately on the same alignment as the northern line of stones for a further 44m and includes seven irregularly spaced stones up to 0.45m high.'
(with permission, from The Secretary of State's Schedule Entry, for Askham Fell Stone Alignment, SM 22526, 7th August 1995.)

Such alignments are thought to have been associated with funeral ceremonies and other rituals and are dated at around the early part of the second millennium BC.

On returning back to the track, notice that the surface changes at a particular point. You are now walking on dry grass on top of a limestone pavement. After about 650ft/200m along from this point, look for a grassy path through the bracken on your left and follow it for approximately 325ft/100m. You eventually reach one of the most impressive Bronze Age monuments in the area: a **Cairn Circle** made of ten large upright boulders **(site 3)**.

Inside the ring of stones is a cairn of small stones with a hollow in the centre. An archaeological excavation of the site revealed an adult cremation with some pottery. One of the finds has been identified as a Yorkshire Vase and is now in the British Museum.

On returning to the track the ground dips and rises, producing several muddy patches before passing between two shake holes followed by an area with shallow **quarries**. After passing a **small cairn** on the left, you will see a solitary standing stone on the horizon. This is the **Cop Stone** **(site 4)**.

Approaching the Cop Stone

Before crossing over to see it, aim off left of the track to find a **shake hole**. Now walk in a straight line from its rim towards the Cop Stone. After sixteen paces look carefully amongst the heather for a finely-branched lichen that looks like a miniature wind-blown tree (its scientific name, *Cladonia arbuscula*, is taken from the Latin word *arbor* meaning 'a tree'). This plant is in fact sold in model shops to make miniature trees for miniature railways!

The Cop Stone was thought to have been part of a second ring cairn with a diameter of over 65ft/20m. There are records going back to the 1880s that recall a circle containing ten large stones laid flat along a stone-filled bank. If you examine the ground north of the Cop Stone you can still see the remains of the circular bank but the recumbent stones are now missing.

This is the furthest point reached on the walk. From here the return journey takes you away from the main track to explore the opposite side. The OS Outdoor Leisure map shows an elongated shake hole with surface water (marked on the map as 'Wofa Holes') but the only suggestion of water that I was able to find in this area was a galvanised water tank that had been dumped there!

Continue along a line roughly parallel with the main track but approximately 500ft/150m – 650ft/200m from it. When you reach a position opposite the Cairn Circle at site 4 you pass two deep shake holes

Bog bean and reflections on surface of water-filled shake-hole

fringed with bracken. Look for a wood **post** near the northernmost hole. You may spot a stonechat along this section. From here, head west across a damp area characterized by heather and sphagnum. With luck you will happen upon a water-filled shake hole covered in **bogbean** – an unattractive name but a beautiful white lace-like flower in June and July.

Make your way back to the main track at the Askham turn-off (passing a **second post** on your right) When you reach the junction (grid reference NY491222) look for a faint path leading off to the west towards a fenced-off area about 330ft/100m up on the left. It is shown on the OS map as the first in a series of deep holes called the 'Pulpit Holes' **(site 5)**.

The wire fence looks promising, but it doesn't prepare you for what is ahead. Here is a deep water-filled crater, complete with island and young willow trees. Throughout this entire walk there have been no trees. Now that you have walked away from the track, you find them safe from grazing in a fenced-off oasis.

In the water there is yellow iris whilst around the edge there are tall clumps of soft rush. It is amongst the rushes that you will find the dragonflies. Look for the 'large red damselfly', darting out like sparks from a fire (its scientific name: *Pyrrhosoma*, comes from the Greek meaning 'fiery body'). Then there are the 'common blues' – the males of which are a striking electric-blue colour. If you are fortunate, you may see one of Britain's largest dragonflies - the 'gold-ringed hawker' with a wingspan of four inches. If it is dull or wet, they will not be flying but you may spot their larval nymphs hunting for beetles under the water.

It is easy to loose direction *en route* to the next site and if visibility is poor, a safe alternative is to return to the track and continue on to the junction of **Ketley Gate** (from here you can join the path leading to the next site by following the signpost left to Howtown). If the weather is clear, follow the line of shake holes leading north-west across the moor until you reach the same path. Suddenly you have stepped off the limestone and onto volcanic rock overlaid with peat. The ground is waterlogged and you find the first signs of flowing water at the start of **Elder Beck (site 6)**.

Notice how the path along here has been made of stones raised above the peat and how the acids in the peat have bleached the rocks white. Immediately after crossing a small stone-slab footbridge, look for a large flat boulder on the right. Geologists call this rock **breccia**. It is made up of chunks of different rocks gathered from around the area and held together in a volcanic glue. The mixture of colours is quite spectacular and is seen at its best when the surface is wet.

Peregrine falcon above Four Stones Hill

Continue over the straight built-up path fringed with rushes until you reach the grassy approach leading up to **The Cockpit (site 7)**. This is the only monument on Moor Divock that has not been built on limestone. It is also the largest individual Bronze Age feature in the area with 27 stones arranged in a 100ft/30m-diameter circle. The path leading to it from the south-west is the High Street Roman Road.

From The Cockpit head north along the continuation of the Roman road. For a brief moment you are on rocks from the Skiddaw Group that extend across from Ullswater. These rocks can be seen in the two **slab footbridges** that cross the tributaries of Elder Beck. The path now climbs back to the **large cairn** where you can turn left to rejoin the moorland track back to the starting point at Roehead.

Site Summary

1. White Raise Cairn (NY489224)
Bronze Age burial chamber with stone cist

2. Askham Fell Stone Alignment (NY493222)
22 stones in two parallel lines extending 230ft/70m in a north-west orientation

3. Ring cairn (NY494220)
Circle of ten large stones with central funeral cairn. Excavated finds include a Bronze Age vase

4. Cop Stone (NY496216)
A large standing stone is all that remains of a 65ft/20m-diameter ring cairn. The circular earth bank can still be seen

5. Water-filled shake hole (NY491223)
Breeding pool for dragonflies and damselflies

6. Peat deposits overlying volcanic rock (NY485224)
Fine example of brightly-coloured breccia

7. The Cockpit (NY483223)
100ft/30m-diameter stone circle containing 27 separate stones

Notes
Historical evidence for a 'serpentine avenue' linking the archaeological sites is discussed in *From Carnac to Callanish: the Prehistoric Stone Rows and Avenues of Britain, Ireland and Brittany* by Aubrey Burl (1993); Yale University.

Two theories have been suggested to explain the formation of shake-holes:
1) The limestone dissolves away underground and the area above catastrophically collapses into it.
2) The surface limestone dissolves away slowly from contact with water at ground level caused by impeded drainage from a raised water-table.

On Moor Divock, the second process is more likely – the shake-holes occupying a distinct band where the edge of the limestone overlies impervious volcanic rock.

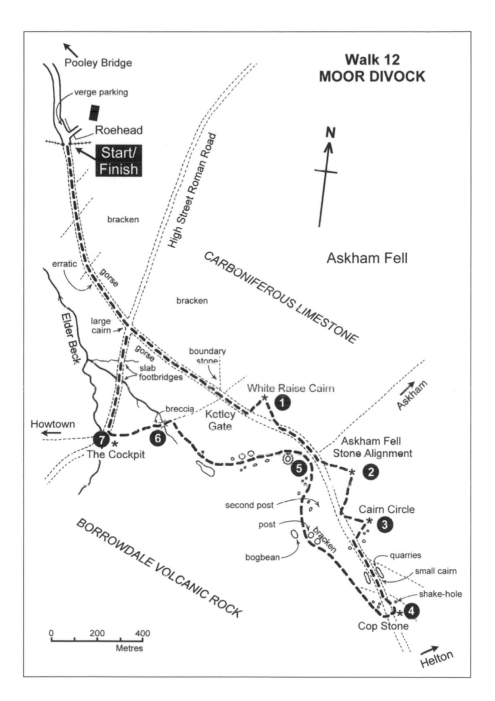

Walk 12
MOOR DIVOCK

Walk 13. Knipe Scar

As you approach from Askham, you know you are entering somewhere different when you have to get out of the car to open a gate on the public road; from the moment you hear the church bell at Bampton Grange chime the quarter.

You are still in the Lake District National Park but this area east of Haweswater is relatively unknown. Few visitors have heard of the place names – Whale and Howgate Foot – and yet this quiet limestone country has a long history of settlement dating back to the Bronze Age.

There are the remains of stone circles and mediaeval enclosures. There are 19th-century limekilns and a limestone pavement with all the wild flowers that you would expect plus the added interest of erratics scattered over its surface.

This is a quiet place to come and get a feel for the past: a place to speculate on how things used to be.

Checklist

Distance	2.1miles/3.4km
Ascent	500ft/150m
Approximate time	2 hours
Maps	1:25 000 OS Outdoor Leisure 5, The English Lakes, North Eastern area. 1: 50 000 OS Landranger 90
Terrain	Gentle gradients over mostly dry grassland
Degree of shelter	Fairly sheltered on the lower slopes of the scar. Exposed along the limestone pavement
Stiles	None
Special considerations	In wet weather, overtrousers are recommended for visiting site 4. The Ring Cairn is an Scheduled Ancient Monument. It is an offence to disturb or deface it or use a metal detector within 6.5ft/2m of its boundary

Footwear	Boots
Parking	There is ample parking space on the grass verge north of the cattle grid (NY522187)

The Route

From the road that crosses Knipe Moor, follow the wall leading up from the cattle grid. This section is sheltered from the south by a plantation of oak, ash and hawthorn. Continue following the wall to where the ground becomes level. In front there is a group of sycamores growing where the wall turns a corner **(site 1)**. You are standing in a shallow depression that runs north-west along the base of Knipe Scar. A short distance from the wall on the left is a rounded stone resting on the finely-grazed turf. It is approximately 1.5ft/0.5m high and has been polished smooth by the continuous rubbing of sheep.

A distant view of Knipe Scar from Moor Divock

Geologists call such stones 'erratics'. They have been picked up and carried by a moving glacier. They lie where they were dropped when the ice melted and their distribution reveals the path taken by the ice-flow. This particular stone at site 1 is composed of Borrowdale Volcanic rock

The blocked doorway. Old maps show a building on this site in 1863

from the central Lake District. It is the first of many erratics that you will see on this walk.

Continue following the wall as it juts out around a curious corner. Look closely at the side of the wall and you will see that suddenly the stones change, becoming larger and carefully dressed. In fact this was once the side of an old building complete with a **doorway**. It has been incorporated into the wall and explains the rectangular bulge in the corner of this field enclosure. A study of old Ordnance Survey maps confirms this. The first edition OS map of this area printed in 1863 shows a building on this site. On the second edition printed in 1899, the building has disappeared.

Follow the wall as it turns right. The prevailing winds are from the west and the wall provides good shelter for the sheep (indicated by the strip of nettles). After 1300ft/400m, turn left away from the wall and climb the slope between **tall bracken**. In front of you there are two limekilns **(site 2)** that appear to have been built at different times. The left-hand kiln is built on a square plan with a Romanesque arch typical of the early to mid-1800s. The right-hand kiln has lost most of its outer wall but the inside 'pot' can still be seen. It is lined with yellow firebrick indicating a later kiln, probably built after 1850. Look closely at the lining and how the silica-rich bricks have almost burnt away in the intense heat of the firing process. Temperatures inside these kilns would reach 1000 degrees Celsius as the limestone was converted into quicklime. A draw-hole at the base was kept open to maintain a constant draft of air to remove the carbon dioxide.

The path at this point may vary depending on the time of year and whether the farmer has cleared a way through by cutting down the tall bracken. Keep parallel with the field walls on your right and once you have reached the top corner, follow the wall closely along a narrow sheep-track. Follow the wall above a line of old hawthorns. All along this section there are thistles, some of which are only found growing on limestone. Look for carline thistle which is quite short with a large solitary straw-coloured head.

Continue along the sheep-track until you reach a **large ash**. Turn left and climb up the grassy slope to a gap in the limestone scar above. On a clear day there are fine views to the south-west to the High Street range. To the north-west, the more-familiar outline of Blencathra can be seen on the skyline. But it is the foreground that holds the eye. This is a classic limestone pavement. There is no definite summit, just a wide promenade of clints and grykes with herb robert, wild thyme, eyebright, wall rue and thistles.

Why are there so many thistles on limestone? The high level of calcium in the soil is one factor. Such fertile land has traditionally been well grazed by sheep which leave thistles well alone whilst removing other competing plants. And perhaps the air currents created by the miniature corridors and canyons over the surface of the pavement encourage the settling of thistledown?

One of the characteristic features of the limestone pavements all

Carline thistle – one of many thistles found on the limestone of Knipe Scar

across northern England is the large number of erratic boulders. There is evidence that many of them were used during the Bronze Age to construct avenues linking cairns and stone circles. Three ceremonial avenues were thought to have been built around Shap and one of these was believed to have extended north in a single row of stones across Knipe Scar. Today only a few isolated stones from these avenues survive and it is almost impossible to know which stones were used for this purpose.

There are a number of erratics scattered over the plateau of Knipe Scar. They are difficult to pinpoint on a map and the lack of any single footpath makes them more likely to be encountered by chance. Even so, a route can be followed to link-up some of the best examples.

Start by positioning yourself midway between the edge of the scar and the wall that runs along the north-east side and follow a route parallel with and approximately 330ft/100m from the wall. This should bring you to your first erratic at **site 3**. It is topped with yellow lichen (the birds choose only the highest points for their look-outs). Other erratics can be found further ahead, all of which show the same lichen pattern.

If you continue parallel with the wall keeping a distance of about 160ft/50m, you should eventually find a wooden post in a small clearing in the bracken **(site 4)**. This marks the site of what was once described as a 'Druids Circle' but is now officially designated as a Ring Cairn. It is very difficult amongst the bracken to find much evidence of this Bronze Age feature. The description from the Cumbria Sites and Monuments Record may help:

> *'An area of broken limestone pavement, some of which appears to have been cleared, the slabs being arranged to form a circle. Smaller stones projecting from the turf between these slabs give the perimeter the appearance of a low bank. In the centre of the circle, which has an internal diam of approx 15m, there is a limestone block. Other blocks are scattered in the SW and NW quadrants.'*
> (with permission, T Clare; MA thesis.)

Continue across the limestone pavement until you reach an area of **cut bracken** where the walking is easier. Look for two circular depressions. These are shallow **sink holes**, often found on limestone where the subsurface has either collapsed or been slowly dissolved.

From the sink holes, head west along the line of the wall until you reach a broad, grassy track that takes you across some exposed pavement and down along to the edge of the scar. Leave the track and follow the edge of the scar for approximately 400ft/120m to reach **site 5**.

Here is a quarried face with a small sycamore and a hawthorn growing out from the top. Scattered along the foot of the rock face are pieces of limestone, some of which contain fossil corals that lived 300 million years ago in warm shallow seas just north of the Equator.

Retrace your steps along the edge of the scar back to the broad, grassy track. Follow this down to a gently-sloping area covered in thistles. You are now at **site 6**: an extensive area of 'ridge and furrow'. This type of cultivation is difficult to date but is likely to have started here in the mediaeval period (11th-16th Century).

The grassy track continues down to High Knipe Farm. Do not take this route but instead turn off left above the field walls and follow the muddy sheep-tracks. Eventually you join a sunken path that leads down between some tall **gorse** bushes.

The ground in front drops gently into a shallow, grassy valley before reaching the road. If the sun is low, you will see the grassed-over walls of an ancient enclosure . It is difficult to know the age of these walls. Some may be contemporary with the Bronze Age features high up on Knipe Scar although they are more likely to be linked with the ridge and furrow markings at site 6. They are certainly much older than the present farm buildings and stone walls which cut straight through them. Follow the road back to your start point.

Site Summary

1. Corner of field wall (NY523189)
Evidence of former building incorporated into stone wall. Volcanic erratic polished by sheep

2. Limekilns (NY527187)
Two kilns of different construction; the most recent has its firebrick lining exposed

3. Erratics (NY529191)
Different-coloured rocks brought here by ice. Possibly associated with Bronze Age 'avenues' linking cairns and stone circles

4. Stone circle (NY529193)
50ft/15m-diameter circular clearing with a limestone block at its centre

5. Quarried face (NY526194)
300 million year old fossil corals found in broken limestone fragments

6. Ridge and furrow (NY524196)
Evidence of ancient cultivation strips on a fertile shelf

7. Enclosure (NY521192)
Rectangular outline of buried walls suggests a long history of settlement along this shallow valley

Notes
Reference to the 'stone avenue' that extends from Shap to Knipe Scar can be found in *From Carnac to Callanish: the Prehistoric Stone Rows and Avenues of Britain, Ireland and Brittany* by Aubrey Burl (1993); Yale University.

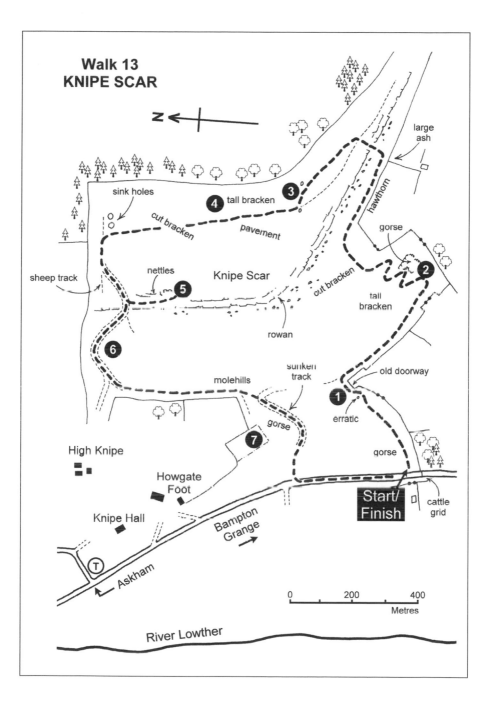

**Walk 13
KNIPE SCAR**

N

large ash

hawthorn

sink holes

tall bracken **3**

4 tall bracket

cut bracken

pavement

gorse

cut bracken

nettles

Knipe Scar

5

sheep track

tall bracken

rowan

6

old doorway

sunken track

molehills

1

erratic

gorse

7

gorse

High Knipe

Howgate Foot

Start/ Finish

cattle grid

Knipe Hall

Bampton Grange

(T)

Askham

0   200   400
Metres

River Lowther

Walk 14. Martindale

Martindale Old Church

By Lakeland standards, few people visit Martindale. There is no through-road and the surrounding hills are not at the top of the fellwalker's list. Those that do venture this far may visit the Old Church and then return to Howtown to catch the Ullswater 'Steamer' or continue back along the narrow road to Pooley Bridge. This has left an area relatively unexplored close to one of Lakeland's busiest centres.

The walk described here is one of the shortest in the book but it highlights a recurring theme of looking at the landscape at close quarters. Martindale is not the place for a route-march. It is a place to slow down and take in the detail – to enjoy those things that are often overlooked in the rush to cover distance.

There is a saying: avoid leaving anything behind except your footprints. Well on this walk, such is its delicate character, there are places where even the footprints are a problem! There is, however, something satisfying in venturing onto 'untouched' ground; in looking without disturbing. For a brief moment you become an explorer, walking into a Lakeland that is virtually unknown.

Checklist

Distance	1.6 miles/2.6km
Ascent	560ft/170m
Approximate time	1 to 2 hours
Maps	1: 25 000 OS Outdoor Leisure 5, The English Lakes, North Eastern area. 1: 50 000 OS Landranger 90
Terrain	Gently-rising quarry path. Mostly dry and without difficulties
Degree of shelter	The cave and church provide shelter from rain. The low-level path is sheltered from strong winds
Stiles	None
Special considerations	Much of the charm of this walk is in discovering a path that is unspoilt and forgotten. Please take care to leave the area as you found it for others to enjoy particularly when visiting the cave. Optional extras that you may wish to take include a hand-lens and binoculars
Footwear	Boots
Parking	There is ample parking space in front of Martindale Old Church (NY434184)

The Route

The focal point of this quiet dale is the **Old Church** of Saint Martin and this is where our walk begins **(site 1)**.

The building in front of you has been here for over 400 years but if you look along the base of the south wall you will see the foundation of a much older chapel built over 700 years ago. But even this impressive history is pre-dated by a far older occupant of the site – 'The Martindale Yew'.

This female tree at the north-east corner of the church has a girth of 19ft/5.8m and is believed to be 1500 years old ('believed to be' because once a yew gets beyond 1000 years it is difficult to date accurately as the inside becomes hollow leaving no continuous tree-ring record). From Celtic times, the yew has been regarded as a sacred tree and its position here would have influenced the building of the first church on this site.

Richard Birkett's tomb below the Martindale Yew

As you stand underneath its massive branches, look for fragments of black feathers and wings on the ground between the wall and the stone tomb. Some years, you may find a dead rook here – often a young bird that has fallen from one of the nests above. The carcass decays very slowly because of the sterile conditions produced by the yew's toxins. This is why (coupled with the lack of sunlight) there is so little plantlife growing on and underneath its branches. No lichens grow here – only a fine green algae that is able to tolerate the tree's chemical defences.

It was therefore surprising to hear of an elderberry bush that had taken root in the crown of the tree. But such is the protection given to this grand old lady – the intruder was spotted and was removed with a chain-saw!

The first recorded curate of the church was Richard Birkett. It is fitting that it is his tomb that takes pride of place under this old yew. He was quite a character and took great care in the upkeep of the churchyard. A visitor to the church in 1688 refers to the *"neat Chapelyard which by the peculiar care and industry of an old yeoman Sir Richard the Reader [Reverend Birkett] is kept clean and neat as a Bowling Green. In which particular he is so very extreamly curiouse that he will not suffer a mole to cast in it but setting all other occasions aside he will watch and kill her with his own hand and if his cow (which doth sometimes graze there) leave any unseamly thing behind her, he will take care to remove it himselfe with all possible diligence."* (from The Martindale Registers; 1633 – 1890).

Before entering the church, take time to study the north wall. Starting at the north-east corner, an old blocked-off doorway can be seen alongside the second window. Further along to the right is a stone carved with the date 1714. This is thought to commemorate the year when many improvements were made including the addition of a flag-stone floor and a porch on the west side.

Once inside the church, notice the small pillar of Penrith Sandstone to the left of the altar. It was brought down from the Roman Road on High Street where it was thought to have been a wayside shrine for the Roman soldiers. It was used by the local dalesfolk as a sharpening-stone and the vertical scratch-marks made by the farm tools and knives can still be seen. Eventually it was taken inside the church and the hollowed-out top supported a basin which was used for baptisms.

After leaving the church and churchyard head north to join the path (**signpost**: Public Footpath) that takes you along the north side of the valley. The soil in this area is very fertile. If you look on the north-east side of the path you will often find **molehills** below the bracken indicating high calcium levels and a large population of earthworms.

The path follows the old wall and after about 330ft/100m passes the ruins of the original **vicarage** on the right. From here onwards you will find many small boulders bordering the path **(site 2)**. The familiar **yellow-topped rocks** are the result of lichens

The font showing signs of its past history

growing on the nitrogen from bird-droppings. For this lichen to grow, a particular rock has to be used regularly by birds as a lookout-perch.

Continue following the wall passing several mature ash trees. The steep fellside on your left is covered in **tall bracken** which indicates the degree of shelter on this side of the valley.

In front is Martindale Forest enclosed by a boundary wall with two gates. Take the left gate. From here, the path is indistinct and great care is needed to ensure to start along the correct route. After counting 20ft/6m from the gate, take a narrow overgrown track which climbs diagonally up to the left. (Do not follow the path that descends slightly right in the direction of The Nab.). The correct path continues to climb gently and 160ft/50m from the gate you pass a large oak on the left. Continue the gentle climb to where the path shows signs of being built-up with stone. At this point, a large **over-hanging hazel** almost blocks the way, but after carefully skirting below its branches, the path can be regained.

The path along this section is built-up as though on a low wall **(site 3)** making the gradient even and regular. This is the first indication that this is no casual walkers' path but a route carefully constructed for pack-horses. But where is it leading?

You pass between two large oaks. The left-hand tree has a **red stone** wedged under its exposed roots. This is a piece of volcanic rock (tuff or ash) that has been coloured by iron.

The path now becomes narrower as it climbs across an open area. After passing a group of hazel and then a large oak on the left, the path narrows once again as you cross another area of open fellside. You may have noticed that each time the path crosses open ground without the shelter of trees, it becomes less distinct. On angles of slope approaching 45 degrees, the soil 'creeps' downwards and tends to hide the path. In the wooded sections, the tree roots and the overhead shelter stabilises the soil and the path is not so disrupted.

You pass a **large sycamore** below the path after which you cross the open fellside for approximately 900ft/280m before reaching a patch of **dead trees** that have been attacked by various insects **(site 4)**. The trees have been killed but they put up quite a battle in their struggle to isolate the attacking intruders. The result is an amazing scene of fallen trunks each one covered in a grotesque pattern of intricate burrs. The rotting wood that remains now supports a raised garden of mosses and wild geraniums.

The cave-dwelling wren

Once again the path can be seen to have been built on top of a low wall so as to ease the gradient and the reason lies just ahead. After a few steps you find yourself standing on the spoil-heap of the Martindale stone quarry **(site 5)**. On the Ordnance Survey 1:25 000 map the quarry is marked as a 'cave'. As you face the entrance, notice the drill holes on each side where the charges were set for blasting. There are wrens nesting here (the scientific name for the wren is *Troglodytes troglodytes* which means 'the cave dweller').

Look inside the entrance. You feel as though you ought to remove your boots before entering! The floor is carpeted with the delicate green leaves of the liverwort, *Conocephalum*. Take a closer look at the top surface of this liverwort, preferably with a hand-lens or by looking through a reversed pair of binoculars. The pattern is caused by air chambers that are compressed into hexagons, each having a large central pore.

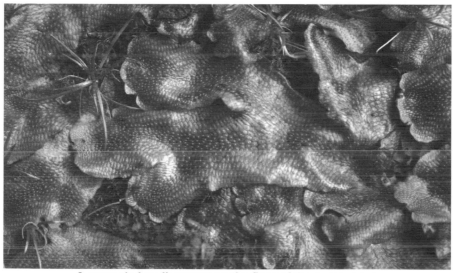

Conocephalum liverwort on the floor of the quarry cave

Another characteristic is the plant's strange antiseptic smell. Normally these plants would grow flat against the rock. But here the forked branches curl up towards the light from the cave entrance. Like flat cartoon characters raising their heads, they could almost be looking back at you as you peer in that them!

The cave marks the furthest point on the walk. Progress beyond here is difficult as the path fades into sheep-tracks. From the cave, therefore, retrace your steps back to the starting point at the Old Church.

Site Summary

1. Church of St. Martin (NY434184)
Famous 1500-year-old yew in north-east corner of churchyard. Sandstone pillar from High Street Roman Road used as a baptismal font

2. Yellow-topped rocks (NY435183)
Lookout-perches for local birdlife showing effects on lichen distribution

3. Engineered path (NY439177)
Path built on low wall to even out gradient for pack-horses. On open fellside the path is hidden because of 'soil creep'

4. Dead ash trees (NY441175)
Standing and fallen dead trees covered in burrs resulting from insect attack

5. Quarry cave (NY441174)
Secluded setting. Damp floor covered in liverwort with leaves curling up towards the light

Notes
An excellent history of Martindale and its churches is given in A *Short History of Martindale* by C N Barrand. This is now out of print but a copy may be seen at the Pooley Bridge Tourist Information Centre.

For information on the Martindle Yew see *The Cumbrian Yew Book*, Ken Mills (1999); Yew Trees for the Millennium in Cumbria.

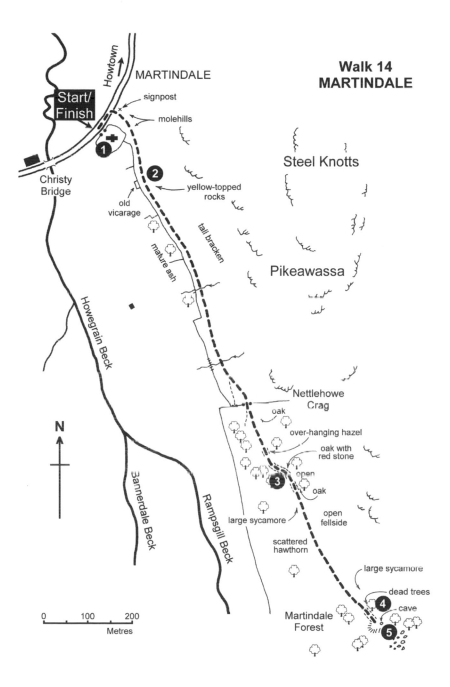

Walk 14
MARTINDALE

Walk 15. Silver Point

One of the most popular outings in the Patterdale area is the walk along Ullswater's southern shore from Side Farm to Howtown making the return journey to Glenridding by 'Steamer'. The shoreline walk, or 'Steamer-link path', is regarded by many as one of the finest in the district.

This particular route goes only as far as Silver Point and returns to Side Farm along the higher bridleway. I first did this walk in June when the lower shoreline path was busy with visitors making the link with the steamer. As soon as I turned off at Silver Point to follow the higher path, I met only one other person – a local lady from Patterdale walking her dog.

This is the perfect circular route from Patterdale if the weather turns foul and you need to get out for a few hours and stretch your legs. The hidden valley between Birk Fell and Silver Crag will be completely new to most people, and its variety of wild flowers is an unexpected delight.

Looking across the flood plane from the bridge south of Patterdale

Checklist

Distance	3 miles/4.7km
Ascent	330ft/100m
Approximate time	2 to 3 hours
Maps	1: 25 000 OS Outdoor Leisure 5, The English Lakes, North Eastern area. 1: 50 000 OS Landranger 90
Terrain	Easy, level path as far as Silver point. The higher return path is more rugged but well-defined
Degree of shelter	A low-level walk, mostly sheltered from the wind
Stiles	None
Special considerations	In extremely wet weather, the path across the fields west of Side farm may be flooded and an alternative approach to the start can be made via the bridge south of the White Lion Inn
Footwear	Boots
Parking	Public car park (NY396159), Patterdale

The Route

From Side Farm follow the farm road heading north along the eastern shore of Ullswater. You pass through patches of mixed woodland keeping the stone wall on your left. The way is dark in places due to the thick canopy of mature beech and sycamore, and because of the shade, the wall has a thick covering of moss. Look for two yew trees growing behind the wall just before you get your first view of the lake **(site 1)**. There is no moss growing on the wall underneath their branches, only a uniform covering of green algae. The yew's toxins would appear to be discouraging the moss and, in the absence of competition, the algae is flourishing.

After passing a clearing with views across the lake, continue on past the camp site. The farm building up ahead on the left has a slate roof and its north-facing side is completely overgrown with moss under the shade of an ash.

Where the path forks right, keep straight ahead. You pass below a walled grass paddock surrounded by tall conifers. After this shaded area where several streams converge, the path becomes narrower with views of open fellside on your right and mature parkland on your left. Eventually the path leads through tall bracken with extensive views of the lake. The wall that you have been following drops down towards the shore on the left whilst the path goes over a rocky outcrop.

You are now standing on a basalt dyke **(site 2)**: a vertical band of once-liquid rock that squeezed its way through the solid surroundings. The red and purple colours are caused by iron oxides. The molten lava was cooled down very quickly and produced a crumbly rock texture. The resulting fertile soil supports a fine group of mature Scots pine.

Continue through the **tall bracken** with patches of juniper and holly on each side. At **Silver Point** bear right over a narrow stream and after a further 330ft/100m take a narrow turn-off to the right marked by a small **cairn**.

You leave the busy Steamer-link path and begin to climb what feels like your own private valley. The path makes its way through a juniper grove along a delightful section that has been constructed over a stone terrace **(site 3)**. There is scree down on your right and steep crags above. The wild flowers in between are exquisite – herb robert, wild thyme, lady's-mantle and wild strawberries. On the loose scree you will find parsley fern. The path then begins to level out as you follow the line of a low wall. Cross the wall and follow the path over a wide grassy level area.

On your left there is a small tarn **(site 4)**. Look below the surface in May or June and there will be dragonfly nymphs hunting their prey. Look closer and you will see tadpoles hiding under the delicate floating water-plants. Further along, the path rises to a wide grassy col. Notice the small rock in front. It is covered in bird-lime tinged purple – a result of the local bird population eating juniper berries. Some places stay in the memory and this secret valley is one of them.

You now descend a broad grassy path. Notice the bell heather covering the crag up on your right. Where the path levels out, look for a prominent **boulder** just off to the right before the bracken begins. There is the usual mustard-coloured lichen covering the top (because of the bird-droppings) but this is also a good place for spotting 'crottle' – a grey, leafy lichen that was used for dying wool. It is one of the few plant dyes that doesn't require a mordent. It provides the brown and gold colours of Harris

Tweed.

The path now follows a pleasant terraced track that was constructed for the use of quarry ponies. The surface has patches of **red basalt** from the same dyke that was crossed on the lower path. The path becomes more stony and passes a group of **hawthorns** and several more streams.

You are now approaching an area of fellside that was extensively quarried for building-stone. Keep a look out for spoil-heaps that mark the entrances. You pass a **small quarry** on the left alongside an ash tree. Several metres further there is a tooth-shaped boulder that indicates the position of a much larger cavern hidden down on the right, below two spreading ash trees.

After passing a Victorian **wrought-iron seat** (notice the date on the backrest), the path drops down over a rough stony section which leads to a narrow quarry on the left **(site 5)**. Just before you reach the opening, notice how the water coming down the fellside stops at the path and turns back to disappear underground. Water also pours over the cave entrance. The quarrying has created a miniature gill and waterfall with a surprising

The path to Silver Point from site 2

Site Summary

1. Yew trees (NY397166)
Effect of yew's toxins on moss and algae

2. Basalt dyke (NY395177)
An intrusion of volcanic rock containing iron (stained purple and red) and supporting fine growths of mature Scots pine

3. Juniper grove (NY398182)
Natural juniper woodland with field layer of alpine flowers including lady's-mantle and wild strawberrry

4. Valley head (NY397179)
Secluded tarn with dragonflies and frogs

5. Quarry entrance (NY398165)
Water-curtain and miniature gill with rich variety of wild flowers and ferns

Notes
For a systematic account of the flora recorded throughout Cumbria see *The Flora of Cumbria*, Geoffrey Halliday (1997); University of Lancaster.

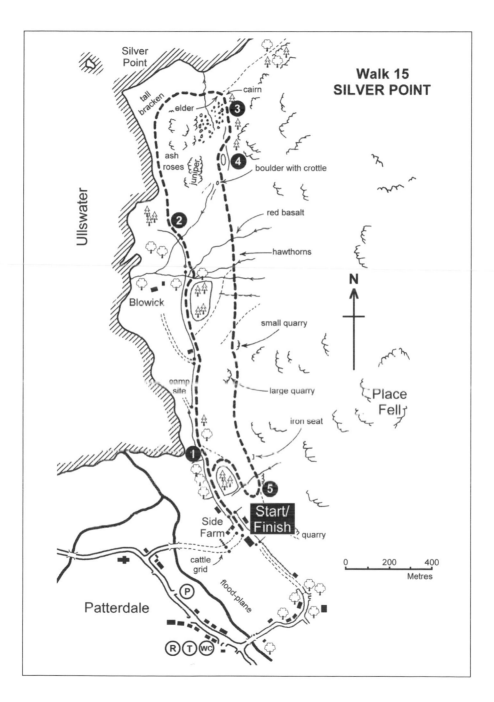

Walk 15
SILVER POINT

Silver Point

cairn

elder

3

tall bracken

ash roses

juniper

4

boulder with crottle

2

red basalt

hawthorns

Ullswater

Blowick

small quarry

camp site

large quarry

N

iron seat

Place Fell

1

5

Start/ Finish

Side Farm

quarry

cattle grid

flood-plane

0   200   400
Metres

P

Patterdale

R T wc

variety of wild flowers and ferns. There is ash, hazel and wild rose. Even the spoil-heap is covered in wild thyme.

Follow the path as it swings sharp right to bring you underneath the pile of spoil. The strange noise coming from below ground is the water that disappeared into the cave above. It finally emerges to cross the path at the foot of the spoil. This section is being colonized by lush growths of brooklime.

Continue along the path until you reach the corner of a walled enclosure where you can drop down left to join the track back to Side Farm.

The path below site 5 swings right, below the quarry spoil
Patterdale can be seen across the flooded fields

Walk 16. Four Stones Hill

Visitors to Haweswater tend to head up the valley to climb the High Street ridges, or walk across to Riggindale to see the golden eagle and the exposed walls of Mardale village. Those walking the north-west shore of the reservoir have their sites set on Robin Hood's Bay. Why else should anyone visit Haweswater?

The path to Four Stones Hill, an ancient Bronze Age site complete with standing stones and ancient cairns, is virtually unknown. The cascading waterfalls, old copper workings and peregrines are passed by. At any point on this walk, you are less than two miles from the Haweswater Dam and yet there is enough here to occupy the keenest archaeologist and birdwatcher for the full day.

This is a walk for those who have 'done' the Lake District and think there is little fresh to discover. When the last 'Wainwright' has been completed, a visit to Four Stones Hill is recommended to show just how much there is still left to see.

Checklist

Distance	4.2miles/6.7km
Ascent	670ft/205m
Approximate time	4 to 5 hours
Maps	1:25 000 OS Outdoor Leisure 5, The English Lakes, North Eastern area. 1:50 000 OS Landranger 90. 1: 250 000 British Geological Survey 54N 04W, Lake District
Terrain	Broad level track alongside reservoir followed by a short rocky climb. The moorland section is mostly dry and grassy but the path is ill-defined in places
Degree of shelter	Good shelter along the tree-lined sections of the reservoir track
Stiles	None

Special considerations	In misty conditions, this walk should only be attempted by walkers who are experienced at route finding using a map and compass. The Bronze Age sites in this area are all Scheduled Ancient Monuments. It is an offence to disturb or deface them or use a metal-detector within a 6.5ft/2m boundary of the feature. The mine shafts at site 5 are flooded and dangerous and should not be approached
Footwear	Boots
Parking	There is space at Burnbanks at the road junction (NY508161). Please do not block the garage entrances opposite the cottages further along.

The Route

From **Burnbanks** follow the signs: 'Public Footpath fellside track via NW shore of Haweswater'. The path takes you past the new houses on the site of the original village (built for the labourers on the Haweswater dam). You path leads under a dark canopy of sycamore to a gate with the open fell on your right *(Please note that the Public Right of Way along this section has been*

The start of the walk at Burnbanks

incorrectly marked on current OS maps). On your left is a thin band of woodland which hides your view of the reservoir until you reach the Heltondale Beck **tunnel** (marked by a slate plaque set in the stone wall). The path continues with intermittent breaks in the trees to your left. Most of these trees were planted after the dam was built and they comprise a strange mixture of evergreens and deciduous including some copper beech. Not until you meet the first bit of original Mardale wall do you find the original Mardale trees **(site 1)**. Here on the right of the path are the more familiar holly, rowan and ash growing together.

A view of Haweswater with the pumping station in silhouette on the far shoreline

As you approach the foot of **Measand Beck** you begin to hear the waterfalls. Cross the wooden footbridge and notice the scent of wood sage (especially if it's raining) that grows by the line of iron posts. Leave the reservoir track and take the narrow path that keeps closely to the left side of the beck. It is steep and rocky in places with intermittent views of the cascading waterfalls and fine views of Haweswater on the left.

You are walking over hard volcanic rock that intruded into the surrounding lavas. Eventually, the path widens and becomes grassy as it levels out. Below you on the right is a sunken dell where the beck flows gently around a grassy island surrounded by wild roses, honeysuckle, birch and willow before rushing through a narrow gorge lined with bell heather. A broad area to the left of the path is fertile grassland. Notice the molehills. The well-drained soil attracts earthworms, and moles eat earthworms.

A little further along and about 50ft/15m to the left there is a large isolated boulder **(site 2)**. There are all sorts of things going on here. This is a favourite perch for kestrels. Look for traces of food pellets on the top. Notice also how the lichens grow in circular zones like concentric bands around a dartboard. Around the outside is dark brown (dark

'After crossing the bridge, a number of tracks fan out in front of you'

crottle); inside is light grey (crottle) whilst around the 'bullseye' is mustard-yellow (*Candelariella*), showing the different concentrations of nitrogen as you approach the centre.

Continue on the level, grassy path to the wooden footbridge **(site 3)**. Look for dippers flying underneath. You may also hear stonechats calling from the surrounding bracken. In clear weather, you will now be able to spot two standing stones on the saddle below Four Stones Hill. After crossing the bridge there are a number of narrow tracks that fan-out in front of you. Choose the one that leads directly ahead as you leave the bridge. This is the path to Four Stones Hill. It is rarely used and has become indistinct in places amongst the encroaching bracken. It keeps to a fairly even gradient in a north-east direction and eventually brings you to the two **standing stones**.

This whole area was once settled during the Bronze Age. Within this one square kilometre, there are 18 listed archeological sites. This was likely to have been a highly successful upland settlement on fertile land during a period of good weather. An analysis of pollen found in the sediments of Haweswater suggests that the climate at that time was much drier than the present day.

The name Four Stones Hill suggests that there should be four standing stones, and a second pair was described in a 1901 publication: *History of the Parish of Bampton* by M E Noble. Here is her description of the scene: *'...two menhirs or standing stones, looking like forgotten gateposts of the roughest description. They are about four feet high, and not set in the ground. Consequently the frequent rubbing of sheep has worn away the ground, and they are now much out of the perpendicular. Two similar stones not far away seem to have fallen from this cause.'* Unfortunately, further surveys since this description was made have been unable to locate the second pair.

The next feature that you pass is the **pool** of water occupying an elliptical hollow to the left of the path. This dries up in the course of a normal summer and if the climate was dry during the Bronze Age, it would have been an unreliable water source. If the water-level is low, you may see a line of flat rocks that have been carefully arranged around the edge, perhaps to minimize the effects of trampling by livestock.

From the pool, leave the path and climb the rough fellside to the top of **Four Stones Hill**. Make your way to the south east edge overlooking the reservoir **(site 4)**. To appreciate the full significance of this spot, you

The standing stones of Four Stones Hill
Only two stones remain of the original four

need to stand here in June with a south-east wind blowing. You will then hear the peregrines: two adults and as many as three young in most years. This is not their nest site, but with the wind in this direction this is one of their favourite slopes for soaring and catching prey. Look at the highest point of the summit. The grass here is a darker shade of green and is littered with food pellets and the remains of small birds. The last time I was here there were a number of pellets measuring up to three inches long that could only have come from a golden eagle further up the valley. This is a place to stay a while and let the wildlife come to you.

A few hundred metres below, there is a beautifully-constructed **tall cairn** on a prominent rock platform (the cairn on Lingmell used to look like this). The skyline in this area is dotted with various cairns, some of which are modern whilst others belong to the same period as the standing stones.

As you walk back towards the standing stones keep a lookout for the remains of a stone shelter built out from the crags on your right. It looks quite old and undisturbed.

Continue past the pool until you reach a large pile of stones. Archaeologists believe this to be a **funeral cairn**. Once again there is the problem of finding modern artifacts associated with those that are prehistoric. In this case, the original Bronze Age cairn has been disturbed in the centre and some of the stones have been used to form a circular shelter.

From the cairn, two tracks lead off in front of you. Take the fainter right-hand path which continues in a north-east direction. Take care here: do not be tempted to turn sharp right, along the rush-lined water course that leads around the east flank of Four Stones Hill.

After crossing a boggy patch with a small stream, you pass through an area of **grass** leading to a damp hollow with rushes. The path follows the stony watercourse (dried up in places) and then crosses it, bearing right along a well-marked path that skirts along the edge of a large area of bracken.

The path you are following now leads across a **marsh** full of rushes and climbs up to the saddle in the crags facing you. Don't follow this. Instead, when you reach the marshy hollow, bear off to the right following the line of the gently-sloping water course. The path is indistinct along this section but aim for a gentle descent through the tall bracken.

You eventually reach a **grassy clearing** in the bracken. Just up to the right through a clump of gorse bushes there is a large area of spoil **(site 5)**. This is the site of one of three copper mines on this side of Four Stones

Hill. Some of the rocks still show traces of the rich copper ore and take on striking refractory colours from orange to purple. The shaft is over 55ft/17m deep, hidden in a thicket of gorse and nettles at the back of the spoil heap. It is extremely dangerous and should not be entered.

Return to the grassy clearing and drop down to join the shoreline path which will take you back to Burnbanks.

Site Summary

1. Mardale trees (NY491157)
Original village wall with local deciduous trees

2. Fertile grassy shelf (NY484156)
Kestrel feeding-perch. Molehills and grey slugs indicate soil calcium levels

3. Wooden footbridge (NY483157)
Dippers flying under bridge and stonechats in surrounding bracken

4. Four Stones Hill summit (NY492163)
Feeding-ledges and soaring-slopes for peregrines and golden eagles. Views down onto Bronze Age cairns and standing stones

5. Haweswater copper mines (NY494161)
Three separate levels (Caution! Deep shafts). Samples of brightly-coloured copper ore found on spoil-heaps

Notes
For an account of pollen analysis and its use in recording the changes in climate in the Lake District since the last glacial period, see *Mountains and Moorlands*, W H Pearsall (1955); The Fontana New Naturalist.

Reference to the Haweswater Copper Mines can be found in *Mines of the Lake District Fells*, John Adams (1988); Dalesman Publications.

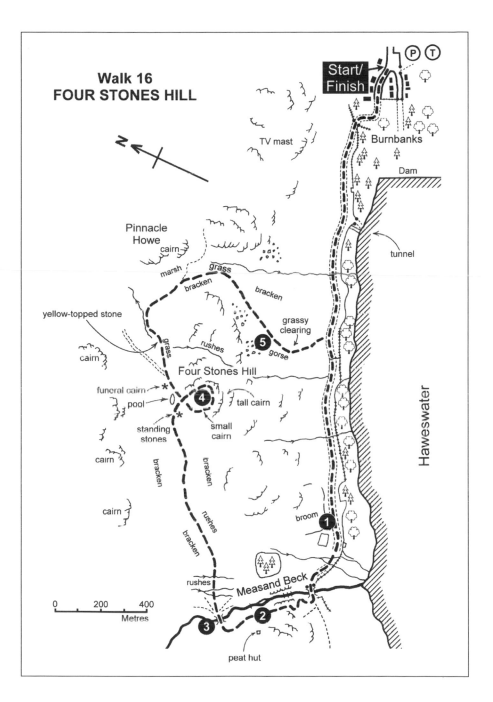

Walk 16
FOUR STONES HILL

TV mast

Burnbanks

Dam

Pinnacle
Howe
cairn

marsh   grass
         bracken   bracken

yellow-topped stone

cairn   grass
                 rushes   grassy
                                clearing
Four Stones Hill   5   gorse

funeral cairn
         pool   4   tall cairn
standing   small
stones   cairn

cairn   bracken   bracken

cairn   rushes   broom   1

         bracken

         rushes   Measand Beck

0   200   400   3   2
         Metres

         peat hut

tunnel

Haweswater

Walk 17. Rydal

Over 200 years ago, Rydal Cave was not a place for holidaymakers to visit. It was a busy working quarry with its own road system for supplying the surrounding villages with building stone. Nowadays, the industry is tourism and the cave is a major attraction. The pool of water at its entrance, once choked with stone slurry, is now crystal-clear and full of fish. The spoil-heaps are colonised by rock plants, and the quarry road is a favourite tree-lined path.

This is a short, gentle walk suitable for young and elders alike. The young will find plenty of places to explore and the elders can tell of plants that eat insects and some that break bones!

Checklist

Distance	2.7 miles/4.3km
Ascent	200ft/60m
Approximate time	2 hours
Maps	1:25 000 OS Outdoor Leisure 7, The English Lakes, South Eastern area
Terrain	Dry footpaths. Mostly level or gentle gradients
Degree of shelter	Very sheltered throughout the entire walk. It may be too sheltered if there are midges about!
Stiles	None
Special considerations	Suitable for all ages and capabilities
Footwear	Walking shoes or boots
Parking	Ample parking space at White Moss Common (NY351065)

The Route

From White Moss Common Car Park head west along the footpath that leads towards the **ford** and footbridge. The path follows the river and then skirts around the shoreline before crossing the large footbridge that takes you over the river connecting Rydal Water with Grasmere.

Approximately 500ft/150m past the bridge on the right you pass a **large beech** with its network of roots raised above the bare soil. Notice how dark it has become. The dense foliage reduces the sunlight and few plants grow here except moss. Without the stabilising effect of grass, the soil quickly erodes away exposing the tree's roots.

The path now starts to climb and goes over an **ice-polished rock**. After skirting around a miniature valley with a small stream running alongside a wall, the path makes it way through the dense woodland until it reaches a gate leading out onto the open fell. Take the path that climbs the slope directly ahead through tall bracken.

After crossing a stream, look for the junction of another path joining in on the right. At this point you should see a large, isolated rock about 65ft/20m to the left **(site 1)**. Take a close look at its west-facing side. There is a line of one-inch-diameter drill-holes. These are similar to the

Rydal Cave

holes found on Kail Pot Crag on the south shore of Ullswater. Certain rocks have a magnetic memory. By taking samples of rock that was once molten but cooled rapidly, geologists can measure the magnetic polarity of the earth from that particular period of earth's history. Look also on the top of this large rock for a small, succulent plant with white star-shaped flowers. This is English stonecrop, clinging to the dry surface of cracks and crevices.

Rejoin the main path, which leads to **Rydal Cave (site 2)**. The large pile of **spoil** below the path is being colonised by stonecrop. Normally this plant would cling to the surface rocks but here in these sheltered conditions, its stems are growing upright, some reaching the dizzy height of 4in/13cm!

The quarry cave is a well-known local landmark, but its size is still a surprise. A series of stepping-stones leads over a deep pool full of fish. Just above the water on a vertical rock face is a patch of 'green' algae that has developed a red pigment. Green algae turn red in bright sunlight. Here, the reflection of the pool's surface doubles the amount of light reaching this south-facing wall.

To continue, cross the stream that leaves the pool and follow the path as it swings down left below the heap of spoil. The path then turns right alongside a fence, passing a group of mature larch before reaching the entrance to a second **quarry**.

Although not as well known as the larger Rydal Cave, this quarry is just as interesting with two cave entrances. The path into it drops steeply down an earth slope with exposed tree roots underneath a sprawling elm. In this sunken hollow, in front of the right-hand entrance, there is wood sorrel, wild geranium and golden saxifrage. But the eye is drawn to the luxuriant ferns that grow characteristically from tight, compact centres. They are known by the rather unflattering name: 'scaly male fern'.

On returning to the path, notice how wide and well-made it has become. This is the quarry road that was used to transport the quarried rock down to Rydal. The section of wire fence that you are following is soon replaced by a stone wall which curves around to the left to cross a stream **(site 3)**. As you reach the corner, notice the large oak on the left of the path. Its branches support fine growths of *Polypody* fern, 16ft/5m above the ground.

The wall is unusual. It has been built so that it butts up to the oak with two neatly-finished stone edges perfectly matching the shape of the trunk. Follow the wall as it curves left across the stream. The water runs under the **quarry road** and emerges from a square hole in the base of the wall.

There is another large tree here which catches the eye. In the bed of the stream is a mature ash. You might expect an alder or a willow to have its feet in water but an ash usually grows in deep, rich soils some distance up from the water's edge. Here it stands in water.

Look at the base of its trunk. There is a bare strip with no moss, lichen or algae. Nothing grows in this narrow band due to the fluctuating water-level. How could such a tree seed itself and take root in the middle of a stream that is regularly flushed through with fast-flowing water? The stream has in fact been redirected during the building of the quarry road. It indicates the amount of earth that was moved at this corner to create a gently-sloping route suitable for quarry ponies. Further along, as you follow the 'road' with its accompanying walls, notice the amount of earth that was used to build up the terraced surface. On some sections you are walking at a height that is above the lower side-wall!

The **quarry road** continues along to a gate where you turn off left to follow the shoreline. **Site 4** is a small rock on the right of the path. All sorts of things are happening here. Firstly, it is a favourite bird-perching site. You can tell that from the usual patch of yellow lichen that characterises such isolated stones. The yellow also extends down to the

The return path along the shore of Rydal Water

Site Summary

1. Isolated boulder (NY350059)
Volcanic rock with lines of drill-holes. Stonecrop growing in cracks

2. Rydal Cave (NY355058)
Large quarry cave with deep pool full of fish

3. Corner of quarry road (NY356058)
Oak built into wall. Unusual position of old ash tree indicates that the quarry road redirected the stream

4. Small rock at side of path (NY359060)
A colony of yellow meadow ants protected by rock. Lichen growth indicates bird perch and 'canine zone'

5. Marshy area (NY352059)
Plants adapted to waterlogged, acid soil: home of the yellow-flowering bog asphodel or 'bone breaker'

Notes
The fish in Rydal cave are minnows that were introduced into the pool by the Freshwater Biological Association (Windermere)

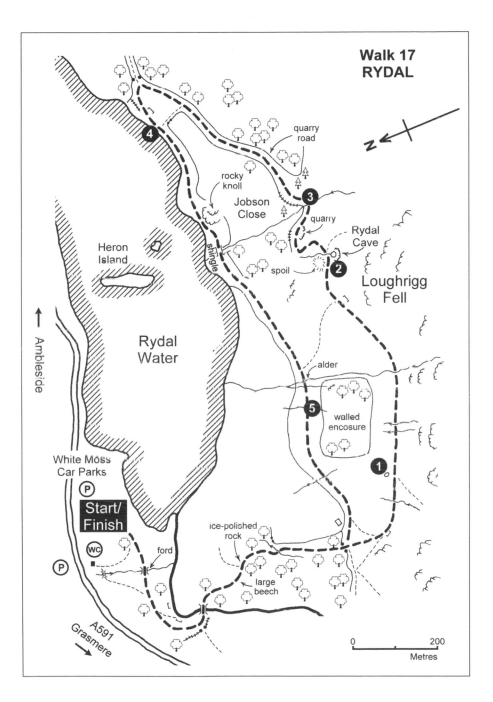

Walk 17
RYDAL

base of the rock but only on the side facing the path. This particular stone is acting as a substitute lamp-post; lichenologists refer to such bands of growth as the 'canine zone'. Look closely at the ground under the warm south-facing side. The brown sandy soil is from an ants' nest. Perhaps these meadow ants favour such positions under stones. As well as offering protection from hungry woodpeckers, the rock acts as a solar panel and heat store.

The path continues along the shore of **Rydal Water**. It is broad and level with the exception of a short section that skirts around the **rocky knoll** below Jobson Close. Where the path crosses a footbridge, have a look at the broad line of **shingle** along the water's edge. On this strandline in summer you will find water mint (purple flowers), tormentil (yellow flowers) and meadowsweet (clusters of small white flowers).

The path is now joined by a wall on the right which leads you away from the shoreline. After approximately 100ft/300m you pass below a **walled enclosure** of woodland. Look for a wide area of marshy grass above the path that is devoid of bracken **(site 5)**. This marshy area has a number of interesting plants that have adapted to living with their roots in water. Here you will find 'cross-leaved heath', recognized by its leaves arranged in groups of four. It is one of the few plants that can tolerate the high levels of iron found in waterlogged soil.

In such waterlogged sites you will also find carnivorous plants, which supplement their diet by eating insects. In May and June look for the blue flowers of butterwort with its starfish-like rosette of sticky leaves.

In late summer, this damp area of marsh will have the yellow star-shaped flowers of bog asphodel (*Narthecium ossifragum*). Quite often in the past, cattle were found with fractured limbs alongside these flowers. The plant was known as the 'bone-breaker' (hence its scientific name: *ossifragum*). Its bad reputation is linked with its habitat. The boat-shaped seeds float on water and often beach themselves and take root along the edges of deep marshy pools – just the place where a cow might get into difficulties. In the past, cattle that grazed on this type of acid moorland would lack calcium in their diet and develop weak bones. Bog asphodel just happens to be one of the few eye-catching plants that grow on calcium-deficient soil. The yellow flower certainly got itself noticed, and the bone-breaker got its name!

The rest of the walk is a pleasant stroll alongside the wall to the gate leading back into the wood. From there simply retrace your steps to the starting-point at White Moss Car Park.

Walk 18. Stock Ghyll Force

Within half a mile of Ambleside's centre there is a Victorian park. In 1890 you would have had to pay an entrance fee of three pence which was increased to six pence by the early-1900s. After many years of legal wrangling and court-cases involving the townsfolk and landowner at the time, free access was eventually restored.

Stock Ghyll Wood is now a Site of Special Scientific Interest (SSSI) and it is possibly the best location in Cumbria to find the rare 'touch-me-not' balsam and the equally rare netted carpet moth. This moth is found only in the Lake District and the larvae feed only on the yellow-flowering balsam.

On a sunny day this is the place to shelter from the heat and escape the traffic of Ambleside's busy streets. On a rainy day it is a welcome outdoor alternative to the shops and cafes... and it's free!

Checklist

Distance	0.75 miles/1.2km
Ascent	200ft/60m
Approximate time	45 minutes
Maps	1:25 000 OS Outdoor Leisure 7, The English Lakes, South Eastern area
Terrain	Well-maintained footpaths with some steps
Degree of shelter	Extremely sheltered throughout the entire walk
Stiles	None
Special considerations	Suitable for all ages and capabilities
Footwear	Walking shoes or trainers
Parking	Ample parking space in Ambleside

The Route

Stock Ghyll Park is traditionally reached by following the road from the back of the Salutation Hotel. The entrance has a gate with iron railings. As you follow the wide, shaded path along the south bank of the river, notice the buildings on the opposite side. They are positioned alongside a **weir** that was once the site of a **bobbin-mill** driven by a large waterwheel. But the water supply was not always reliable and the owner resorted to steam power:

> *'The ugly, tall chimney behind [the waterwheel] is a memorial of the drought of 1859. The owner of the mill suffered so severely from want of water to carry on his trade, that he determined no other summer should find him unprepared with a more reliable power.'*
> (Guide to the Lake District of England by Herman Prior, 7th ed. 1890)

After approximately 200ft/60m, the path takes you over a small stream. Where the path forks, keep right until you reach a narrow, **ivy-clad bridge**. The path now makes its way between some mature oaks towards a Victorian viewing platform **(site 1)**. Notice the iron railings that have been so carefully constructed complete with overhead arches. Today such artificial restraints may seem strange but during the early 1900s when the Lakes were becoming popular, they were thought essential for the safety of tourists and especially for those *'enthusiasts with the camera'*, who are warned not to climb over *'lest they get into trouble, as one at least of the fraternity once did'* (The English Lake District; M.J.B. Baddeley, 13th ed.).

**Netted carpet moth on
touch-me-not balsam**

Return to the main path. In summer this area is dark because of the surrounding beech trees. In front of you is another section of iron railing. It is anchored to the trunk of an oak tree **(site 2)**. Three bars of iron have been embedded into the trunk. The tree has responded by producing extra layers of cells under its surface and the result is a strange bond of metal and wood like three swollen knuckles. The oak is producing tannic acid which is slowly dissolving the iron at the junction. (Incidentally, this is why oak furniture is usually made with brass fittings rather than iron which would corrode away.).

Continue climbing until you reach a path junction in front of a picnic-table. Take the path to the right which leads to the upper exit fitted with an elaborate iron turnstile **(site 3)**. Originally, during the time when payment was charged to see the falls, this turnstile would have had a ratchet mechanism, allowing for exit but not entry into the park. Take a closer look at the top of the wall on the left. It is

A view of Stock Ghyll Force from the safety of the iron railings '... lest enthusiasts with the camera get into trouble.'

covered in *Polypody*, a fern that is usually found growing high up on the branches of trees.

On retracing your steps back to the junction, you pass an old wooden seat below the path. There are many seats within this woodland. All of them were positioned looking out over a particularly good view, and this seat was no exception – only the wood has since grown and the view from here has long gone.

On returning to the junction, turn right up a series of steps. The pink flower growing over the log to the right of the steps is a wild form of geranium called 'herb robert'. Cross the wooden footbridge onto the north bank of the river. Look for a tree stump on the left of the path **(site 4)**. It is covered in a the fan-shaped brackets of *Trametes* fungus.

Follow the path as it drops steadily and look for a small side-path that curves back towards the river to the viewpoint at **site 5**. This is arguably the best view of Stock Ghyll Force. (You may have noticed the variation in spelling of Stock Ghyll: whenever the word 'ghyll' is used instead of 'gill',

Site Summary

1. Viewing platform (NY383046)
View of falls with elaborate iron railings and arches

2. Oak tree (NY383046)
Three iron bars embedded in tree trunk causing unusual growth in the tree's outer layers

3. Iron turnstile (NY383045)
Exit to woodland. Entry was restricted to the lower gate where Victorian tourists were charged an admission fee

4. Tree stump (NY385046)
Fan-shaped growths of *Trametes* fungus

5. North-bank viewpoint (NY383046)
Good view of Stock Ghyll Force. Samples of 'hard fern' with upright, fertile leaves growing alongside path

Notes
The guide books by Herman Prior and M J B Baddely from which the quotes are taken can be seen in Ambleside's Armitt Museum and Library.

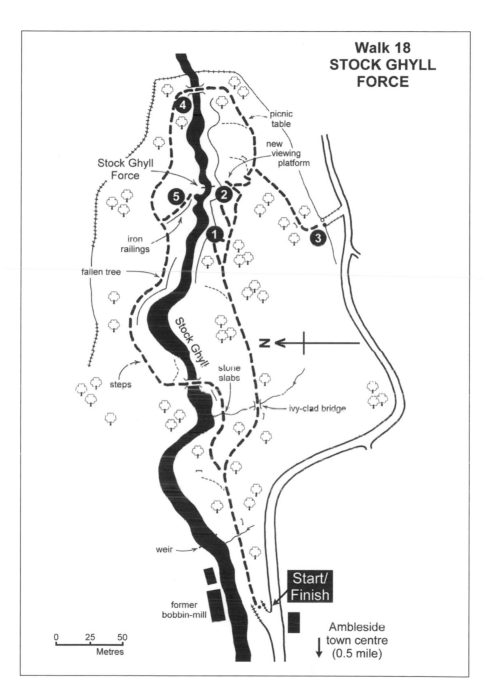

Walk 18
STOCK GHYLL
FORCE

picnic table

new viewing platform

Stock Ghyll Force

iron railings

fallen tree

Stock Ghyll

steps

stone slabs

ivy-clad bridge

weir

former bobbin-mill

0 25 50
Metres

Start/ Finish

Ambleside town centre
(0.5 mile)

it has usually been retained as a carry-over from Victorian times, indicating its popularity with tourists of that period.). The height of the fall is officially 60ft/18m although 100ft/30m has been quoted in some earlier guides.

The iron turnstile at site 3

As you return to the main path, notice the bank of vegetation on the right. Here are a number of leaves that look like the backbones of fish. These are the fertile leaves of a fern called 'hard fern'. If you look on the back of the leaf in summer, it will have rows of spores. The leaves lying flat against the ground belong to the same plant but look entirely different and produce no spores.

Continue following the main path along the north bank. After descending a series of steps, you cross a wooden footbridge and then some stone slabs before returning to the path that takes you back to the starting-point.

Walk 19. Kentmere

There is something strange about the shape of Kentmere Tarn. Most Lakeland valleys were formed by glacial action leaving a symmetrical lake in a scooped-out hollow. The term 'ribbon lake' is often used to describe the long thin outline with parallel sides. But Kentmere Tarn looks more like a ribbon with a knot tied in it.

It wasn't always so. Up until the 1830s, 'Kentmere' as it was known, could have been mistaken for a miniature Coniston Water. And then in 1840 it was drained in the hope of providing new land for farming. The result was an acid marshland.

The reason for the poor drainage was a layer of silica-rich plants called diatoms whose remains formed a continuous layer across the valley bottom. When the economic value of this material was realised, it was extracted by dredging the land and a new tarn was formed. Today, the diatomite industry has gone leaving this quiet stretch of water to the local swans and the occasional fisherman.

Checklist

Distance	4.9 miles/7.8km
Ascent	525ft/160m
Approximate time	4 to 5 hours
Maps	1:25 000 OS Outdoor Leisure 7, The English Lakes, South Eastern area
Terrain	Fairly level well-defined paths for most of the way except for the moorland section between sites 6 and 7 which is boggy in places
Degree of shelter	Very sheltered along the woodland sections but exposed on the moorland alongside Park Beck across to Whiteside End
Stiles	1 (optional, alongside gate)

Special considerations	Navigating the moorland section alongside Park Beck can be difficult in mist
Footwear	Walking shoes or trainers (in dry weather)
Parking	There is limited parking space for 6 or 7 cars outside the Church Hall (SD456041)

The Route

This walk begins and ends at **Kentmere Church**. Follow the farm road heading west towards Kentmere Hall. The road drops gently until you reach an elder tree on your left. You are now standing on the shoreline of what used to be the 'mere' of Kentmere. The flat land that you see over the wall on your left was covered in water before it was drained in 1840. The shore followed the 158 metre contour-line which is roughly the course of the farm road you are now walking.

After passing the elder tree, look out for an unusual mixture of national plants: Scottish harebells on the right and Welsh poppies on the left. You are now in a slight hollow which acts as a frost-pocket. Just before the road bends slightly right, it crosses a field-drain **(site 1)**. This insignificant-looking water channel used to be the main inlet for water entering the mere.

In order to get the full picture we need to go back to a time of former global warming, about 5500-3000 BC, just after the last ice age but before the main deposits of peat were laid down. At that time there were two lakes in the valley: the lower one occupying the land over the wall to your left; the upper one out of sight to the right, midway between here and the Kentmere Head Reservoir. The shore of this forgotten lake followed the 226m contour-line and was as large as Buttermere.

What happened to this lake? It used to drain quietly through the gap between Rook Howe and Raven Crag (see OS Outdoor Leisure 7) following the line of the drain in front of you. But there was a second outflow at its south-east corner and this eventually cut through a soft dam of loose moraine. The increased water flow of this emerging river (the River Kent) continued cutting through the underlying rock creating a much-lower outlet at the Force Jump waterfall (north-east of the Church) and the lake above simply drained away.

It is interesting to note that during its existence, the upper lake acted as a filter-bed for the lower lake and it was this, coupled with the warm

The field drain at site 1. This was once the main water channel connecting Kentmere's former lakes

climate, that provided perfect conditions for the growth of diatoms in the lake below.

Continue along the road with **Kentmere Hall** now clearly in view. You pass through two gates and then turn left through a gate in the corner of a wooden fence (sign: Public Footpath Only. No Bicycles Please). The path crosses a grassy field with a plantation of trees fenced-off on the right **(site 2)**. Here in the summer months you will find clusters of white flowers on long stems growing along the edge of a stream. This is meadowsweet, once used as a cure for headache. It contains the chemical salicylic acid, more commonly known as aspirin.

Go through another gate following the path across a concrete **ford** and through two more gates. A few hundred metres ahead of you on the left you can see a smooth grassy mound framed between two prominent trees. This is Lunsty Howe which is marked on some maps (as is Whirl Howe in Longsleddale) as though an ancient barrow or tumulus. It is unlikely that this is a burial mound as it is situated below the former shoreline and therefore would have been partly submerged at the time when such mounds were being built.

The path now climbs gently and leads through a gate into Hall Wood containing mostly sycamore with the occasional birch and coppiced hazel. You emerge from the wood through a gate into open grassland. 330ft/100m further on the left of the path you reach a large boulder **(site 3)**. This is a major landmark for the local population of ravens. All the signs of bird activity are here: the mustard-coloured lichen on top, and rock tripe on the vertical surface below. You may also find raven food-pellets, regurgitated in the manner more associated with owls. And like owl-pellets, they will show what the birds have eaten recently. When I was last here in mid-August, they contained seeds of corn and the hard wing-cases of assorted beetles.

The path you are walking follows the old shoreline. The 'new' shoreline of **Kentmere Tarn** can be clearly seen below. After a gate, you enter an area with scattered hawthorn and hazel. About 160ft/50m past the gate on the left is an old, coppiced ash **(site 4)**. You are now just above the level of the old shoreline and this tree would possibly have been part of a coppiced hedge along the water margin. Look carefully at the horizontal branches that fan-out just above ground level. On the right-hand branch are two varieties of dog lichen. Carefully peel back the leafy structures

Looking across to the 'new' shoreline of Kentmere Tarn

and note the Velcro-like white barbs that attach it to the mossy surface (please do not remove). The spores are produced on chestnut-brown crescents at the ends of the leaves.

The path continues along the old shoreline. After a stile, the route becomes narrower as you enter a more enclosed woodland. You pass a gate on your left (sign: private fishing), and then an old iron shed, hidden in the trees. Look carefully for a path that cuts off to the left to a concrete platform at the water's edge **(site 5).**

This is where the diatomite was lifted out of the water and transported by aerial ropeway. The foundations for the support pylons can still be seen. Along the edge of the concrete platform is a line of iron posts that held a safety chain. The former lake bed was dredged using a drag-line to scoop out the diatomite and the shape of the new tarn followed the path of the grab-bucket as it was pulled along a line from north to south.

Rejoin the shoreline path and continue until you reach the former **diatomite works**. There are few walks in the Lake District where the atmosphere changes as quickly as this. Suddenly you emerge from woodland into an industrial wasteland. The path runs alongside a huge concrete yard enclosed by a 10ft/3m-high retaining wall

The concrete platform at site 5 where diatomite was brought ashore

made of railway sleepers. This is the terminus for the aerial ropeway where the dredged sludge was dumped and left to drain before being 'calcined' in a kiln. As recently as the 1970s this yard would have been completely filled with grey earth ready for processing into diatomite. Production continued until 1985.

Kentmere was one of the few sites in Britain where diatomite was worked commercially (the other main centre of production was the Isle of Skye in the early 1900s). Over 70 different species of microscopic diatom have been found in British deposits and when processed they can contain up to 98% silica. Diatomite (or kieselguhr) was added to nitroglycerine to make it safer by absorbing the unstable liquid and transforming it into dynamite. It was also used as an abrasive in the manufacture of toothpaste.

For the biologist there is little to be found on this site except to note the extraordinary growth of cup lichen on the sides of the old sleeper walls. What is interesting is that these lichens are extremely healthy despite growing on wood that was once treated with creosote. Perhaps decades of contact with absorbent silica has removed the toxic creosote from the wood surface.

The path now takes you through a modern factory complex. After leaving the works entrance, look for a gate with a sign: 'Kentmere Pottery', leading along a narrow side-road. The pottery is situated at Sawmill Cottage. Look for a millstone with the date AD 1722 carved on it. Between here and Staveley there were at least ten water mills taking power from the River Kent. After the mere was drained in 1840, the flow of river water supplying the mills became so erratic that in 1848 a reservoir was built at Kentmere Head in order to stabilise the flow.

After passing the pottery buildings keep left following the narrow path with **iron railings** on each side. This takes you between some well-kept gardens to a footbridge. Cross the bridge and follow the walled lane to a T-junction and turn right (**signpost**: Public Bridleway Kentmere Hall 2.5 miles). The path is enclosed by walls and in August and September there are some excellent wild blackberries to be found on both sides.

A gate leads into the open fellside with a large sweet-chestnut tree growing alongside the wall on the left. About 160ft/50m in front on the left of the path you pass a group of small ant-hills (home of the yellow meadow ant, *Lasius flavus*). A few metres further above the path is a large isolated boulder **(site 6)**. This is almost the same situation found at site 2 where a particular rock takes on great significance for the local birdlife and farm animals. All the signs are here: the yellow lichen on top; the bird-droppings and food-pellets – and the polished surface used as a rubbing-post. The east-facing side is overhanging and provides a favourite back-scratcher for the sheep. Notice that the grass has been worn away directly below.

The route now follows a sunken pathway leading gently uphill, bearing left at an old **ash** and then right after passing a **rowan**, the path continues to climb gently. Notice the large number of ant-hills on each side where sections of stone wall have been grassed over and the ground is well drained. On the skyline up ahead on the right are three **cherry trees** growing as though planted in a row. The middle one is dead but still standing. The path continues to climb and leads past a deserted cottage and walled garden before crossing the ford at **Black Beck**.

Once over the beck, continue through the gateway in a wall and follow the grassy path with bracken on each side. If the weather is clear, there are good views behind down the Kent Valley with Williamson's Monument prominent on the right. Approximately 330ft/100m after crossing the stepping-stones over Park Beck, the path curves left following a bulge in the stream **(site 7)**. The heather growing alongside the path is cross-leaved heath (*Erica tetralix*) and is able to tolerate the waterlogged conditions. Its mauve flowers develop in mid-summer and the more sunlight the petals receive, the darker they become. Look on the shaded underside of each flower and you will see that it is much paler than the surface exposed to light.

The path stays above the winding tributary of Park Beck. Do not cross over. Instead, follow the path through a gate and climb gently keeping closely to the left side of a wall that will lead all the way back to Kentmere Hall. This wall is a major landmark. It is part of the ancient boundary wall of Kentmere Park, thought to have been enclosed in the 16th Century.

After contouring around the crags of **Whiteside End**, the path begins to drop steadily. You pass through a complicated series of gates and sheep pens, after which the path drops more steeply past a **transmitter mast** and the disused **Parkbrow Quarry**. Some of the blue slate gravestones outside Kentmere Church came from here. The slate is also to be found in the walls bordering the path up ahead. Notice the fine growths of maidenhair spleenwort found growing almost exclusively on the shaded north-east-facing sides.

Just before crossing a small stream, you pass a large alder tree on the left and then a strange-looking ash over the wall on the right. The ash has had its top sawn off and just below the cut surface is a clump of soft rush that is managing to grow in a wet hollow 10ft/3m above the ground.

As the path drops down through the next gate, there is a fine view of Kentmere Hall with its 14th-Century pele tower. Down to the right of the path, you pass a large sycamore. This is a most accommodating tree. Notice the young rowan that has taken root in its branches and the rooks nesting up above.

Site Summary

1. Field drain (SD454042)
Course of water channel connecting Kentmere's two former lakes

2. Fenced plantation (SD452041)
Extensive area of meadowsweet along the water's edge

3. Isolated boulder (SD454033)
Lookout-perch for ravens. Zones of lichen indicating effect of nitrogen from bird-droppings

4. Former Kentmere shoreline (SD455027)
Old, coppiced ash with dog lichens

5. Dredging platform (SD455025)
Site of aerial ropeway for removing diatomite

6. Isolated boulder (SD453016)
Lookout-perch for rooks and rubbing-post for sheep

7. Bend in river (SD443025)
Waterlogged peat deposits with cross-leaved heath

Notes
For information on the former lakes of the Kentmere valley see *Principles of Physical Geography*, F J Monkhouse (1971); pp.203-205. University of London Press.

A history of the Kentmere valley from the Stone Age to the present can be found in *A Lakeland Valley through Time*, edited by Joe Scott (1995); Stavely and District History Society.

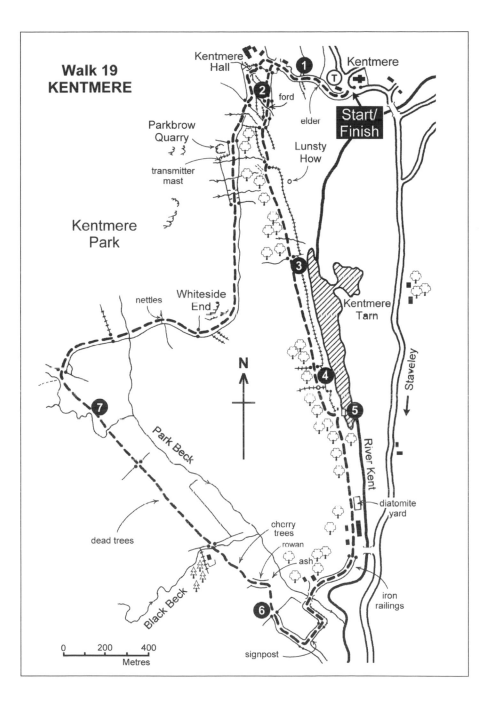

**Walk 19
KENTMERE**

Kentmere Hall

Kentmere

ford

elder

Start/
Finish

Parkbrow
Quarry

transmitter
mast

Lunsty
How

Kentmere
Park

nettles

Whiteside
End

Kentmere
Tarn

Staveley

N

Park Beck

River Kent

dead trees

cherry
trees

rowan

diatomite
yard

ash

Black Beck

iron
railings

0   200   400
Metres

signpost

The path takes you across a low, concrete footbridge. A few metres past the bridge on the left over a wire fence is a tree sometimes mistaken for a sycamore. Its more compact leaves are those of the field maple (*Acer campestre*) – the only true British maple.

You are now back at the farm road outside **Kentmere Hall**. Retrace your steps back to the church. If you have time, it is worth while visiting the churchyard to see the yew tree. This fine tree used to have two trunks held together with an iron chain, but now only one trunk remains. Its girth has been measured at 15ft/4.5m which would suggest an age of up to 600 years.

Walk 20. Cunswick Scar

Many visitors intent on walking the Lakeland hills will pass through Kendal without thinking of walking the Kendal hills, leaving this outlying countryside for the locals to enjoy. The area does not form part of any long-distance footpath. Neither does it form any direct walking-link with the rest of Lakeland. Scars are often isolated by farmland and their linear nature means that they do not have walks developed as Horseshoes or Rounds.

Walking on limestone offers an alternative experience. Most of the scars on the south-east edge of the Lake District are SSSIs and none is more easily accessible than Cunswick Scar. Here is a complete contrast to the Central Fells and a chance to see why such outlying areas have been labelled 'Sites of Special Scientific Interest'.

Checklist

Distance	3.6 miles/5.8km
Ascent	360ft/110m
Approximate time	3 hours
Maps	1:25 000 OS Outdoor Leisure 7, The English Lakes, South Eastern area
Terrain	Mostly dry lanes and footpaths. Level well-drained grassland on top of scar
Degree of shelter	Sheltered along the lower woodland sections
Stiles	3
Special considerations	Please keep to the public footpaths when passing Cunswick Hall
Footwear	Boots
Parking	Public car park at the top of Underbarrow Road (SD489924)

The Route

This walk starts at the car park between Scout Scar and Cunswick Scar on the Underbarrow Road. The first thing to notice if the weather is wet is the slipperiness of the car park surface. This is a limestone pavement and rainwater is continuously dissolving its surface leaving a thin film of calcium salts which acts as a lubricant.

From the car park, take the path through an ash and hazel wood that leads past the trasmitter mast to a gate (signpost: 'Public Footpath Cunswick Fell'). The path follows the wall around the edge of a field, passing another signpost. The limestone pavement is never far below the surface and is exposed in certain places. This type of grassland is one of the richest in the area for its variety of wildflowers. Look for wild thyme, harebells and spear thistle amongst the grass, and herb robert on the stone outcrops.

Scattered around the field are hawthorns that have been grazed by cattle. Grazing encourages side-shoots to form. The trees are no more than columns of short twigs, some of which are less than 3ft/1m high!

The lime kiln at site 2

As you follow the wall, and just before the overhead electric wire crosses it, you reach a group of trees growing against the wall side. You pass an elder, a yew and then an ash. Approximately 170ft/50m further, the path goes alongside several small outcrops of limestone pavement near a scrubby hawthorn **(site 1)**. Look carefully around the rock margins for the yellow flowers of lady's bedstraw and the white, compact florets of yarrow. When I was last here, one of these rocks had been used as a thrush's anvil with fragments of snail shells scattered over its flat surface. This particular snail, *Cepea nemoralis*, has alternate brown and yellow bands and is commonly found in limestone areas: snails need calcium to make a shell.

Follow the wall past more grazed hawthorns until you reach Gamblesmire Lane and turn left through the gate. Notice the benchmark on the right-hand post about half a metre above the ground.

The lane descends between scattered hawthorns and ash and then a right-hand fork leads to a lime kiln **(site 2)**. Such kilns are found in large numbers in limestone regions on both sides of the Pennines. Over 270 kilns have been recorded recently in the parishes of Sedbergh, Garsdale and Dent.

The front chamber has a Romanesque arch and a magnificent barrel-vaulted ceiling (notice the fine growths of maiden-hair spleenwort). This is a good place to shelter in heavy rain.

Most of these square kilns were built in the early 1800s. Hidden within the square structure is a 'pot' about 6.5ft/2m in diameter and 10ft/3m deep, shaped like an egg-cup with a draw-hole at the bottom. The pot was filled with alternate layers of limestone and fuel which was lit from below. The fire would burn slowly for three or four days, converting the limestone to quicklime. Temperatures inside would reach 1000 degrees Celsius which meant that the firing-chamber of unlined kilns frequently crumbled and had to be rebuilt.

Retrace your steps back to the path-junction and continue along the lane. After passing through a gate, the track follows a field wall **(site 3)**. On your right there is a single oak and then a row of sycamores – and this presents us with a puzzle. Take a close look at the wall. It is covered in moss except for one section below the overhanging branches of the oak which has a bright yellow lichen. The lichen's name is *Xanthoria* from the Greek word for yellow. That's the easy bit! The puzzle is: why does it grow under the oak and not under any of the ash?

At the end of the row of trees, turn right to follow the field wall. A signpost (Public Footpath) indicates the way through a gate and the path continues with the wall now on your left. After passing a section of wire fence that bulges out from the wall look for a dead ash leaning out over the wall **(site 4)**. It has been attacked by a bark beetle, leaving an elaborate pattern of radiating channels.

Elaborate galleries left by bark beetles at site 4

The path continues alongside some farm buildings until you reach a gate leading onto a muddy farm track. Do not turn left (this leads to **Cunswick Hall**). Keep straight ahead with the wall on your left for 200ft/60m and then a gate leads out of the field and onto the farm road.

The path follows the field wall on your right, crosses a cattle-grid and then goes over an electric fence. After 980ft/300m, turn right at a yellow waymark, through a gap-stile into Ash Spring Wood. This dark wood is mostly sycamore and beech. The name 'Spring' refers to a coppiced woodland and a number of the original coppiced hazel can still be seen along the southern boundary. The path leads to a second gap-stile taking you out of the wood and into a field. On my last visit here, this field was full of young partridges that followed me around, expecting to be fed!

There is no clear path across this field but make your way to a gate in the wire fence that encloses the woodland opposite. Once through the gate the path follows the line of an old wire fence with woodland on the left and open marsh on the right. After crossing a stile, the path immediately forks. Be careful here to take the left-hand path that climbs up between the ash and hazel.

This is a magnificent limestone scar wood (**site 5**) that is hardly visited even in the summer. As you climb between the limestone outcrops, you find plants that are refreshingly different from those found in central Lakeland. At a level section, you cross a farm track and continue straight ahead. Look for a **spring** on the left of the path with the remains of a low retaining wall. Where the path becomes steep, look for two **yews** on the left and notice how there is very little plantlife growing underneath. Their dense foliage effectively keep out the sunlight. Elsewhere, below the sycamore and hazel, there are wild strawberries, herb robert and hart's-tongue fern.

The path now makes its final climb to the top of the scar through parallel bands of limestone and more yew. The top is reached through a gate in a wire fence. Turn left to follow the path along the edge of the scar.

Keep a lookout for scattered bird feathers all along this section. This is a favourite haunt of peregrines that take advantage of the open space above the trees to bring down their prey.

The path goes through a passage lined with gorse, bramble and hawthorn: Goretex-wearers beware! Look for a juniper along this section. It is full of berries, some green and some the more familiar black. Juniper berries take two years to mature and change colour.

Juniper berries take two years to mature and change from green to the more familiar black

The path follows the edge of the scar on a level with the tops of yew, hazel and whitebeam growing on the limestone ledges just below. On a clear day, the walk along the edge of the scar to its north end (**site 6**)

Site Summary

1. Limestone outcrop (SD492927)
Thrush's anvil with lady's bedstraw and yarrow

2. Lime kiln (SD492929)
Well-preserved example with Romanesque arch. Spleenwort growing on the underside

3. A lichen puzzle (SD488931)
Does the type of tree and the prevailing wind direction effect the plant-growth on this stone wall?

4. Group of dead trees (SD486932)
Radiating pattern left by wood-boring beetle under bark

5. Scar Wood (SD491938)
Quiet woodland with ash, sycamore and yew. The field layer includes wild strawberry and hart's-tongue fern

6. Viewpoint (SD491943)
Extensive views from top of scar over Kentmere and south-east Lakeland

7. Limestone scree (SD492939)
Loose rocks containing fossils of solitary corals

Notes
The dead ash at site 4 has been attacked by the ash bark beetle, *Leperisinus varius*. The adult bores a hole down below the bark and then tunnels across the wood grain to form its egg galleries on each side of the entrance tunnel. Eggs are laid at regular intervals on opposite sides of the tunnel. The newly-hatched larvae then create evenly-spaced feeding galleries that follow the wood grain (perpendicular to the egg galleries). The larvae pupate in a swollen 'cell' at the end of each tunnel from where the new adult bores its way out to the surface

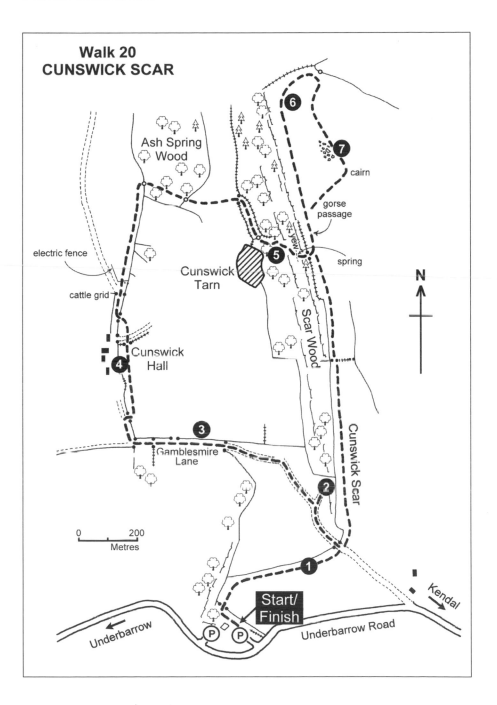

**Walk 20
CUNSWICK SCAR**

Ash Spring
Wood

electric fence

cattle grid

Cunswick
Tarn

Cunswick
Hall

Gamblesmire
Lane

Scar Wood

Cunswick Scar

cairn

gorse
passage

yew

spring

N

0   200
Metres

Start/
Finish

P   P

Underbarrow

Underbarrow Road

Kendal

provides excellent views across to Kentmere and Longsleddale and the dry, level surface makes for easy walking. Amongst the grass, look for carline thistle and small scabious.

After reaching the north end of the scar, return along the high ground visiting the loose pile of limestone scree scattered below the west-facing slope **(site 7)**. Some of these stones contain fossils – mostly solitary corals that once lived in the sea 300 million years ago.

Make your way past the groups of yew and ash to the highest point on the skyline, marked by a small **cairn**. Looking west from here you can just see the outline of Cunswick Tarn over the edge of the scar. From the cairn, drop down to rejoin the path along the edge of the scar. You pass the gate where you first emerged from above the woodland and continue with the fence on your right. The path wanders between gorse and various forms of stunted yew and prostrate juniper. All along this section there are anthills built by the yellow meadow ant. Some are 30cm high indicating well-established colonies in undisturbed grassland.

Ant-hills of the yellow meadow ant on the return path from Cunswick Scar

Follow the path through a gate in a wire fence and continue on to Gamblesmire Lane from where you can retrace your steps back to the car park.

Also from Sigma Leisure:

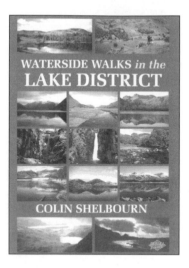

Waterside Walks in the Lake District
Colin Shelbourn

25 stunning walks along the shores of some of the most beautiful lakes to strolls beside rushing rivers and wild water- falls. Whatever the length or location you choose you'll meet with stunning scenery, a richness of wildlife, and many interesting places to visit.
£7.95

Lake District Natural History Walks
Case Notes of a Nature Detective
Christopher Mitchell

18 walks suitable for all ages and abilities Fascinating facts help you interpret the country- side by looking at the effects of geology and plant life on the animal population of the area.
£8.95

Walks in Ancient Lakeland
Robert Harris

Discover stone circles, standing stones and burial cairns. Follow ancient trackways and explore largely unknown areas to uncover the mysteries of the lives of our ancestors. Accurate sketch maps guide you to sites in valleys or the wild and remote fells.
£6.95

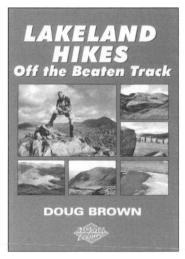

Lakeland Hikes
Off the Beaten Track
Doug Brown

This is for walkers who enjoy a challenge, like to test their navigational skills, want to use their GPS and locate interesting landscape features. Doug Brown has found many remote and unusual routes, with optional exciting scrambles.
£7.95

Best Pub Walks in the Lake District
Neil Coates

This, the longest-established (and best-researched) pub walks book for the Lakes, is amazingly wide-ranging, with an emphasis on quality of walks and the Real Ale rewards that follow!
£7.95

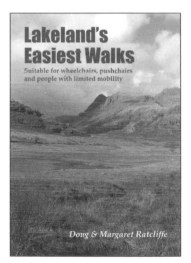

Lakeland's Easiest Walks
Suitable for wheelchairs, pushchairs and people with limited mobility
Doug & Margaret Ratcliffe

These 38 specially selected short walks are all equally suitable for people with limited mobility and for very young children.
£7.99

Walking the Wainwrights
Stuart Marshall

This book links all 214 peaks in the late Alfred Wainwright's seven-volume Pictorial Guide to The Lakeland Fells. Clear route descriptions are presented with two-colour sketch maps.

"An excellent, concise manual on how to tackle the 'Wainwrights' in an intelligent way." – A. Harry Griffin MBE
£8.95

The World of a Wainwright Bagger
Chris Stanbury

Chris Stanbury provides an insight into the world of a 'Wainwright Bagger', inspiring those new to The Wainwrights, to those who have done most of the fells with a series of essays giving a flavour of the enjoy- ment to be found in completing Wainwright's 214 fells.
£8.99

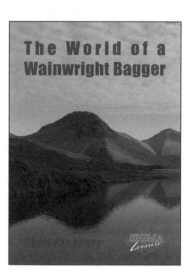

Walking In Eden 2nd Ed.
Ron Scholes

A book to guide you through this forgotten wilderness in 30 circular and direct walks which illustrate the rich variety of walking in Eden. The text includes outline route maps, attractive photos and line draw- ings to convey the feeling of this remote and attractive area.
£8.95

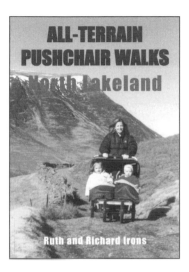

All-Terrain Pushchair Walks
North Lakeland
Ruth and Richard Irons
30 walks from Ennerdale Water to Lowther Park and from Haweswater to Bassenthwaite. There's something for every type of walker. Ruth and Richard Irons are experienced parents and qualified outdoor pursuits instructors.
£6.95

All-Terrain Pushchair Walks
South Lakeland
Norman Buckley
30 graded walks from level routes around pretty Lakeland villages to the more advent- urous (but safe) hikes across the windswept hills. Whatever the age of the family here is the ideal opportunity to escape into the wide-open spaces.
£7.95

Lakeland Walking on the level
Norman Buckley
Walk among the highest mountains of Lakeland and avoid the steep ascents – with no compromises on the views! *"A good spread of walks"* – Rambling Today.
£8.95

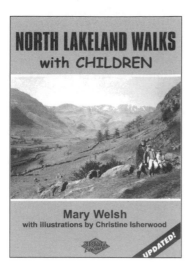

North Lakeland Walks with Children
Mary Welsh; illustrations by Christine Isherwood

"It has been great fun speaking to children I have met on the walks and listening to what they have to say," says Mary Welsh. Written specifically for parents of reluctant walkers.

£8.95

South Lakeland Walks with Children
Nick Lambert

"With Nick Lambert's lively commentary, there seems little likelihood that recalcitrant children will be bored or fratchy."
– The Keswick Reminder

£8.95

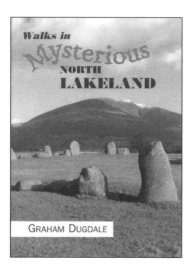

Walks in Mysterious North Lakeland
Graham Dugdale

30 walks to places with a strange and mythical history. *"Each walk features remarkable hand-drawn maps and stylish, entertaining writing that is almost as good to read before a roaring open fire as on the open fells."* – Lakeland Walker

£6.95